PADRE PIO
THE SCENT OF ROSES

IRISH MIRACLES AND CURES

COLM KEANE

CAPEL ISLAND

Copyright Colm Keane 2013

First published in Ireland in 2013

by

CAPEL ISLAND PRESS
36 Raheen Park, Bray,
County Wicklow, Ireland

ISBN 978-0-9559133-5-8

No part of this book may be reproduced or transmitted in any form or by any means without permission in writing from the publishers, except by a reviewer who wishes to quote brief passages in connection with a review.

Printed and bound by Clays Ltd, St Ives plc
Typesetting and cover design by Typeform Ltd

For Seán

Colm Keane's 23 books include the four number one bestsellers *We'll Meet Again, Going Home, Padre Pio: The Irish Connection* and *Nervous Breakdown*. He is a graduate of Trinity College, Dublin, and Georgetown University, Washington DC. As an RTÉ journalist, he won a Jacob's Award and a Glaxo Fellowship for European Science Writers. His books, spanning ten chart bestsellers, include the recently-published *The Distant Shore* and *Forewarned*.

CONTENTS

1. PREFACE — 1
2. INTRODUCTION — 3
3. EARLY YEARS — 12
4. MIDDLE YEARS — 69
5. LATER YEARS — 127
6. ACKNOWLEDGEMENTS — 212

Pray, hope and don't worry.

Padre Pio

PREFACE

The scent of roses has been associated with Padre Pio since the stigmata, or 'wounds of Christ', appeared on his body in 1918. It is often likened to the smell you might get from a garden of roses in bloom. Many people describe it as 'the most beautiful perfume imaginable.' It is also normally associated with the news that prayers are being answered.

Often referred to as the 'aroma of paradise' or 'odour of sanctity', this intense, sacred smell was identified at an early stage as coming from Padre Pio's wounds. It has been further narrowed down to emanating from his blood. It was likewise noticed that it lingered on his clothes and on the bloodstained mittens and bandages he wore.

For those who have experienced this celestial fragrance, it is sometimes said to persist like a steady summer breeze; other times, it comes and goes. People on continents far away have smelled it and known that he was there. It has been remarked upon by devotees, fellow friars and by medical experts who enquired into his extraordinary physical condition.

No one has identified what causes the fragrance. Nor is it confined to the smell of roses; some people describe it as being like lilies, violets, carnations, incense or tobacco. What we do know, however, is that it has heralded numerous miracles and cures. Because so many of the narratives in the chapters ahead testify to this, Padre Pio's 'scent of roses' has been given the prominence it deserves: as an integral part of the title of this book.

INTRODUCTION

On his travels throughout Italy, shortly after the end of World War II, the distinguished Irish author Seán O'Faoláin witnessed a most startling event. The Cork-born writer had just arrived in San Giovanni Rotondo, near Foggia, in the sun-baked boot heel of Italy, hoping to meet an unusual Capuchin friar named Padre Pio. Since 1918, the friar had not only borne the five wounds of Christ but had cured the sick, appeared simultaneously in multiple locations and demonstrated an extraordinary capacity to read people's minds.

As O'Faoláin waited at the old weather-worn chapel, the bearded Capuchin, then aged 62, brown-robed and brown-eyed, suddenly appeared, beating a path through the surging crowd on his way to hear confessions and say Mass. Directly in front of him, and blocking his way, was a sallow, keen-eyed youth. Without even pausing, Padre Pio cried out in Italian, 'Begone, Satan!' The youth, as O'Faoláin put it, wavered, paled and slunk back into the mob.

Later that day, O'Faoláin met the young man and asked about what had happened. He said that he was a clerk from Milan, an agnostic, a true non-believer, who had undergone a serious operation the previous year and had only come to San Giovanni to appease his mother. Curious to see what the friar was like, he was standing there, looking and saying nothing as Padre Pio approached. 'I can tell you he frightened me when he said, "Begone, Satan!"' he remarked, 'I do not know how he knew that I am an agnostic.'

There were many mysterious things relating to Francesco Forgione, or Padre Pio, that puzzled and energised the public, clergy and medical profession following his rise to prominence in 1919. His ability to see into people's souls was just one of them. Further strange attributes, including the gift of prophecy, bilocation and ecstasy, were also identified in the very first article written about him, which appeared in May 1919 in Italy's influential daily newspaper, *Il Giornale d'Italia*.

Other Italian newspapers were quick to follow suit and write about this man they referred to as a 'saint.' In June 1919, *Il Tempo* revealed how he had healed a soldier whose gangrenous foot was determined by doctors to be untreatable. That same month, the Naples-based *Il Mattino*, in a full-page feature, reported yet another miraculous cure. Within a year, Britain's *Daily Mail* was describing to its readers how people were flocking to San Giovanni to see this holy man.

A few decades later – towards the end of World War II, as the Allied forces advanced up through Italy – the first Irish visitors arrived in San Giovanni to seek out Padre Pio for his blessings. Stationed in nearby Foggia, Irish airmen and ground troops, serving with the British armed forces, wound their way to the nearby mountaintop monastery in search of the curious friar with the wounds of Christ. Among them was Belfast-born RAF chaplain Fr. P. Hamilton Pollock, who would eventually become prior of the Dominican community in Limerick.

On his first visit to San Giovanni, Pollock entered the local church to pray. 'One of the brown-robed priests was kneeling in front of the high altar,' Pollock wrote in his autobiographical account of the war, *Wings on the Cross*. 'His cowled head was

INTRODUCTION

inclined forward, his hands buried deep in the loose sleeves of his habit.' Wishing to enquire where Padre Pio might be found, he walked up the aisle of the church and tapped the priest on the shoulder.

On the third tap, the covered head, which had been absorbed in prayer, looked around. Staring into what he described as Padre Pio's 'beautiful face,' Fr. Pollock remarked how, at the moment he disturbed him, he recognised that Padre Pio 'was very far removed from this world' and he knew straight away that the owner of the face 'was not of this earth.' Having established an immediate rapport, 'the saint and the sinner walked out of the church, arm in arm,' Pollock recalled.

On Fr. Pollock's recommendation, armed forces personnel were allowed to attend Padre Pio's Masses and witness the stigmata. 'His hands were beautifully chiselled as if made of white marble,' Pollock observed. 'The fingers were long and tapering, with half-moon nails. In the middle of each hand was a large raw open wound, sometimes covered with congealed blood. Towards the end of Mass, which lasted for two hours, the troops would pour into the sacristy and there they were privileged to kiss the bleeding hands before Padre Pio covered them with swabs and brown mittens.'

Irish soldiers and airmen returned from the conflict to their homes throughout Ireland with spellbinding stories of their meetings with this curious friar. They described his mystifying wounds, extraordinary Masses, mysterious aromas, miraculous cures and remarkable conversions. They also told extraordinary stories of how this intensely devout man could read souls and appear in multiple locations at the same time. The Irish public, which was staunchly committed to the faith, was mesmerised.

Fr. Pollock, fresh from his many encounters with Padre Pio,

traversed Ireland lecturing in a vast array of venues including Dublin's Mansion House and Gresham Hotel, Limerick's Stella Ballroom and Royal Cinema, and a multitude of town halls and school auditoriums throughout the country. The information and images he imparted were riveting: how he saw and kissed Padre Pio's wounds; how Canon Law forbade Padre Pio from wearing gloves at Mass, thus ensuring his stigmata could be seen; how at the Consecration he appeared to be on the cross; how he weighed 12-and-a-half stone and his hair was steel-grey.

Irish Catholics were deeply enthralled. The *Donegal News*, as early as 1949, featured a report on the friar's health, pointing out how 'the wounds on his hands, feet and side remain open and bleed constantly.' The *Ulster Herald*, in the early 1950s, noted important events in his life. He was discussed on Radio Éireann. Books profiling his life were published, vying with works from the popular fiction writers of the era like Agatha Christie, Edgar Wallace and Leslie Charteris for space on bookshop shelves.

So prominent was Padre Pio's profile that, in the wake of World War II, the esteemed Cork-born writer Seán O'Faoláin worked his way to San Giovanni to meet with the future saint, becoming one of the first post-war Irish pilgrims to do so. He arrived at a tiny village boasting little more than a dusty piazza, a few trees, a 500-year-old monastery which was once a hermitage in the wilderness, and where 'pilgrims hung about as patiently as dray horses' while waiting for the holy man to come out, hear confessions and say Mass.

During his visit, O'Faoláin was introduced to the friar, a person he described as an 'ordinary, healthy, grizzled, stoutish,

Introduction

middle-aged, tired-looking man,' with an unquestionable and unforgettable magnetism. 'When I spoke to him he became jovial, almost hearty, laughed with pleasure when he heard that I was Irish and laid his two hands warmly and affectionately on my head in benediction,' O'Faoláin later wrote in his book *South to Sicily*. 'Thousands have spoken to him, found him, as I did, kindly and jovial, amiable and kind, and because his humanity is so evident his saintliness is all the more impressive.'

With interest growing fast throughout Ireland, commercial pilgrimages were soon being put together to enable the Irish faithful to travel to San Giovanni. As early as 1953, Gerry Fitzgerald, who was proprietor of the Palm Grove Café in Limerick city, proposed the first of these visits. In 1956, 72 pilgrims departed from Belfast's Clonard parish. Joe Walsh Tours, which was established in 1961, offered 10-day trips, costing 59 guineas, with pilgrims travelling on comfortable Viscounts. So well-received was the company's first venture, in October 1961, that the booking list was closed five weeks in advance. Mairead Doyle, a Dubliner who had befriended Padre Pio in the 1950s, also ran tours. Many of those who travelled ended up receiving mentions in the local or national press.

Irish journalists flocked to Italy, too. They were transfixed by Padre Pio's early Mass, held at five o'clock each morning. Stella Collins, writing for the *Irish Independent*, described the pandemonium in front of the chapel: 'The seething masses crushed and pushed amid the admonitions of the men and cries of women in the crowd. Eventually the door was thrown wide open and the swaying masses fell forward towards the church. We gained admittance as best we could and then all of us scampered to the Altar of Saint Francis at the right-hand side of the church. We found a chair, placed it in position and sat down with a sigh of relief.'

Lauri Duffy, reporting for *The Irish Press*, recalled Padre Pio's demeanour during Mass: 'His every movement appeared to be painful. When he genuflected it seemed as though a heavy cross weighed him down. He rose with great effort. When he turned towards the congregation and extended his hands the reddish brown scabs on his palms were plainly visible. Many gasped when they saw these marks for the first time. A trickle of blood from the wounds on his hands is often seen by those near enough to him. These wounds can only be seen when he is celebrating Mass.'

Patricia McLaughlin outlined her vivid impressions, also for *The Irish Press*: 'I expected to see an emaciated man and instead I saw an old monk, of robust build, with a beautiful ethereal face – the face of a man whose soul truly transcends the frightful suffering of his human body. He was immaculately robed in white and gold and the whiteness of his face complemented the whiteness of his hair. At the Consecration the poor helpless hands held the Sacred Host. Here was Golgotha brought home to each and every one of us as never before.'

Fr. Adrian Lyons, who was put up in the monastery and who slept three rooms down the corridor from Padre Pio, provided further images of the Mass for *The Kerryman*: 'At times, he seems agitated, as if he were looking out over a world laden down with sin and misery. At times, tears course down his cheeks. Again one notices the lips moving as if in intimate colloquy with Christ. Amongst the congregation there is no sign of restlessness. Nobody seems to get tired or bored or leaves.

Introduction

Occasionally, somebody close by can be heard sobbing quietly.'

The visiting newspaper columnists also honed in on Padre Pio's confessions, which marked the other main preoccupation of his earthly vocation. Lauri Duffy observed: 'This is still his principal activity and he passes much of his day in hearing confessions. So great is the demand that, when I was there, it was necessary to have one's name on a waiting list. In the case of men this meant waiting about a week. For women there was a three weeks delay. Many penitents have personal experience of his power to read souls.'

Fr. Adrian Lyons likewise wrote about Padre Pio's famous confessions, focusing first on those for men: 'According to a general Italian custom, they are heard in the sacristy. They kneel on an open prie-dieu beside Padre Pio. The women are heard in the church in the confessional, on which is that simple name: Padre Pio. Let it not be thought that he is a kind of "refuge of sinners," what is often called an "easy" priest. He deals with souls individually. With some he can be unsparing in severity, in his remarks and retorts. He is quite capable of making people wait for days before giving them absolution. The physical toll of the confessional is at times clearly visible on his face. On it one can see effort, even exhaustion.'

As the 1960s progressed, the trickle of Irish visitors to San Giovanni developed into a steady flow. They were drawn by Padre Pio's simplicity and his genuine holiness; attributes that contrasted sharply with the remoteness, solemnity and stiffness of religion at home. He offered empathy and compassion, bore pain and suffering with quiet dignity, worked miracles and, in doing so, brought hope. He liked the Irish, remarking at one stage that 'Ireland is a country beloved by God.' In turn, the

Irish saw him as one of their own; a living saint with a direct link to heaven.

His intense love of prayer also proved popular. 'Never grow weary of praying,' he frequently remarked. Although he initiated a network of approved prayer groups in Italy and elsewhere as far back as 1947, they were slow to take off in Ireland. On many occasions, he suggested to his friend and devotee Mairead Doyle that she should set them up. Inspired by her, the first formal group was established in 1970 at the Pro-Cathedral in Dublin, with many more eventually coming to life elsewhere in the country. A central Padre Pio office was also inaugurated in Dublin in the late 1970s.

By the time that the Irish prayer groups and office were established, however, Padre Pio had gone to his eternal reward. Since 1967, his five wounds had been gradually disappearing and by summer 1968 only dry crusts and a pink redness were discernible on his hands. On 23 September 1968, after a spell of failing health, he passed away just days after the fiftieth anniversary of receiving the visible stigmata. Padre Pio's earthly mission had come to a close.

It seemed fitting that on the week of his death many Irish pilgrims had arrived in San Giovanni either separately or as part of organised tours. One group, led by Mairead Doyle, had the privilege of a special interview with Padre Pio, who conveyed his blessing and presented them with mementoes of their visit. They were still in Italy when he died. Another tour, led by Tom Cooney, from County Clare, departed for Italy on 28 September, five days after the friar had expired.

'He was very old and also very frail,' Kay Thornton, from County Dublin, a pilgrim who attended one of Padre Pio's last Masses and funeral, recalled. 'He was hardly able to move.

Introduction

He had to be helped on to the altar. He was sitting down during the Mass. He stumbled on the way back into the vestry and someone had to catch him. We were there for the funeral. I kissed him laid out in the coffin. It was unbelievable how many people were there. It was very special.'

On 26 September 1968, the casket containing the body of Padre Pio was placed in an open hearse and driven slowly through the crowded streets of San Giovanni. The journey of little more than three miles took in excess of three hours. More than 100,000 mourners, some of them women dressed in black and kneeling down, lined the route. Many cried, 'Long live St. Pio,' anticipating the elevation to sainthood that was yet to come.

'After my death I will do more,' Padre Pio had promised many times. Emphasising the point, he had often stressed that his real mission would only begin then. What precisely he was referring to is anyone's guess. There is no doubt, however, that the miraculous cures and life transformations following prayer to him formed part of his prophecy, as no saint is more inextricably linked to revivals from incurable maladies or from personal adversities than Padre Pio. From that perspective alone, as the following stories testify, he was certainly true to his word.

EARLY YEARS

In November 1962, a Polish psychiatrist named Dr. Wanda Poltawska was diagnosed with an intestinal tumour. The prognosis was grim. Her doctor said it was 95 per cent certain that the tumour was malignant. She was also told that, even if she came through surgery, she would have 18 months to live at best. She had a choice to make: to go under the knife or not. With four children to rear, she opted for surgery.

One of her close friends at the time was Karol Wojtyla, a fellow Pole and bishop who would eventually become Pope John Paul II. He was distraught when he heard the news. Having befriended Padre Pio in 1947, when he had visited San Giovanni as a young priest, Wojtyla wrote a letter asking for prayers for his friend. On reading the letter, Padre Pio said, 'This is impossible to refuse.'

Dr. Poltawska was listed for surgery on a Friday. On the Saturday, Wojtyla telephoned her family to see how it had gone. He spoke to her husband, who informed him that she had been sent home early, before the procedure was scheduled to take place. Fearing the worst – that the operation had been cancelled because the tumour was inoperable – Wojtyla began to console him.

Dr. Poltawska's husband interjected, saying that it wasn't like that at all. Instead, he said, the doctors had discovered prior to the operation that his wife's tumour had disappeared.

Early Years

That's why she was sent home. 'Wanda no longer has cancer,' he explained. 'They could not find anything.'

At the time of that extraordinary event, many Irish people were turning to Padre Pio either out of curiosity or seeking help for their illnesses and maladies. Some were praying to him from afar; others were making their way up the dusty road leading to the friary of Our Lady of Grace in San Giovanni Rotondo. The years from the 1950s to the end of the 1970s were busy ones in Ireland's devotion to the future saint, as the following stories reveal.

Mary O'Connor, from Cork, recalls meeting Padre Pio in the 1950s. She is now in her late 80s.

My son had a serious operation just after he was born in the 1950s. We only had a slight hope that he would be alright. At the time, my sister-in-law mentioned a man named Padre Pio, who was new to the world. I remember saying, 'I saw a book about him in the local bookshop.' I had stopped and looked at it, but I hadn't bought it because it was a little bit beyond my means in those days. My husband said, 'Don't worry. I'll go down and buy it.'

That's what my husband, Dan, did and he read it from cover to cover. He got very interested in Padre Pio after that. He eventually said, 'I think I'll go out to Italy and see that man.' He hadn't an idea how to get there, but he went anyway. He travelled on his own, going overland. It was a long and difficult trip in those days.

The only person he knew of in San Giovanni was Mary Pyle, who was an American devotee of Padre Pio who lived there and who dealt with Padre Pio's English correspondence. Dan went straight to her and he told her about himself. She looked at him and she said, 'You're very lucky because another American, named Joe, who was a G.I. during the war, is here. He knows Padre Pio and he will help you. I'll put you in his hands.'

Joe brought Dan to meet Padre Pio. At the time, following devotions, Padre Pio used to meet a few people who were picked out to see him. Joe took Dan to where the meetings took place and told Padre Pio who he was and where he had come from. Joe then told Dan, 'Kneel down and you will get Padre Pio's blessing.' That's what Dan did.

Dan could never remember that blessing. He was so struck with Padre Pio that he just knelt down and went off into a trance. He knew that Padre Pio blessed him and that he put his hand on his head, but he couldn't remember anything else. Afterwards, he was completely taken by Padre Pio. I will always remember, after he came home, he said to me, 'We will go out there next year or the year after, if we can afford it, and we'll bring our two boys with us.'

As Dan suggested, off we went to San Giovanni with the two boys and Dan's sister and brother, who had both decided to go with us. At that stage, Dan had got to know Fr. Alessio, who cared for Padre Pio and who had come to Cork. Dan had met him in Cork and he made contact with him again in San Giovanni. It was during that trip of mine that I first encountered Padre Pio.

I first saw him when he was hearing confessions. It was amazing to witness. People were actually coming along and pulling his hands out of the confession box. I thought it was desperate. At times, he could be very cross, especially at Mass if he thought people weren't taking enough interest, and that's how he was that day. You could hear him giving little shouts from inside the confessional.

I was waiting outside the confessional, along with my son. My son was a bit restless, but I had bought some sweets at the airport on the way out and I found a big, red sweet in my pocket which I gave to him. He sat there, sucking it, and he was delighted. The memory of that sweet, after so long a time, stays with me.

The next thing, Padre Pio came down from the confession box, which wasn't far away. He gave me his hands to kiss, he put his hands on my head and he put his hands on my boy. I looked into his face and I got an awful fright. He looked supernatural. He was different from any other living being I have ever seen. He literally shone and his eyes were remarkable. He was pale-featured, but he had a glowing expression.

The whole thing had a huge effect on me. I was so startled that I handed over the child to my husband and I ran out of the church. I ran down the hill and I was hysterical. I worried that I had offended God all my life. I felt, 'If God is anything like Padre Pio, how could I have ever offended him?'

We went over to San Giovanni many times after that. I was there for his Masses, which were always crowded. I remember Dan warning me, 'Get to the church early and go up near him.' On one occasion, I went down very early and got up near the top of the crowd outside the church waiting to get in. Soon, the local women were coming in droves. The more that came, the further back you'd be pushed.

There were so many there that when the door swung back, the fellow who was opening it from the inside had to swing back with it. That morning, I got up to the third row. All of a sudden, the women lifted me out of my seat. I got an awful fright. They were local Italian women and they were very possessive. They thought they owned him. I ended up at the back of the church.

I saw him doing christenings, with the babies wearing little tea cosies. I can also remember him at devotions, where he would turn around with the monstrance in his hand and he would look at it and you'd know he was seeing God. You'd know he was picked out as a symbol to the world that there is a God there.

I saw him do a marriage as well. I even once remember, after he finished his Mass, he was up in the gallery, kneeling and praying, which he often did. A couple were getting married and they came down the church. As they did so, Padre Pio stood up in the gallery, looked over the banister and blessed them. What a beautiful thing to do!

We also visited San Giovanni in 1968, on the night when Padre Pio died. We brought our own children, plus some other children, with us on that visit. We took the plane to Rome and the train to Foggia and then travelled to San Giovanni. I remember we arrived at 12 o'clock at night only to be told by the hotel receptionist that they had no booking for us. I nearly died. They eventually got us a room and we got to bed very late.

The next morning, we got news that Padre Pio had died during the night, a few hours after we had arrived. The only thing I said was, 'He's suffered so much and he's gone to heaven.' Dan said, 'Let's get the children up and dress them and we'll go up to the church and see what's happening.' When we got there, there were lots of policemen and they were putting up barriers. His Italian women followers were arriving already. I thought, 'God! What are we in for?'

Dan said, 'We'll go up to the door of the church,' which we did. We knew no Italian, but I said to the guard, 'Padre Pio! Irlanda! Bambinos!' Believe it or not, he opened the door and let us in. There were crowds already inside. We went up near the altar and there was lots of activity going on, involving policemen, friars and priests who had clearly just come from Rome.

Padre Pio's body was already there, in his coffin, up in the altar area. Dan handed two of the children who were with us to a policeman, who in turn passed them over to kiss Padre Pio. We wanted to have our own child kiss him, too. We took him to a priest and asked him would he lift him in where the coffin was. He did, and what did the boy do only lift Padre Pio's hand!

I then said to Dan, 'Would you please stay with the children? I want to get nearer to Padre Pio.' I went to the back of the altar and I got in. As I got there, they were changing all of the candles on the coffin. I asked the priest, 'Would you mind giving me one of the candles?' He gave one to me. Pieces of it have gone all over the world. A neighbour of mine has the last bit of it next to her bed. She is unwell, so I told her to keep it.

I always pray to Padre Pio to this day. He is part and parcel of me. We always had a photo of him up in our shop. We had a photo up in the kitchen as well. Any time we went out to San Giovanni, we took hundreds of letters with us. I have also heard so many stories of miracles he performed and we would spread devotion to him as much as we could.

I can still see him to this day, especially his eyes and his expression. There is no doubt that he was near God. He was linked to God and he was oblivious to everything else. He was, and is, a great miracle worker. I will never forget him, especially his face on that first day I saw him. There's no way I could ever forget that. I can still see him as clearly as if he was just coming down the aisle.

JOHN COYLE, FROM COUNTY DOWN, recollects his father's early visit to San Giovanni to see Padre Pio.

My dad Sean, who was born in 1917, and his sister Gabrielle, who was older than him, travelled to San Giovanni in the mid-1950s. My dad had studied the piano from a very early age and was a full-time musician. He was a concert pianist of some repute and used to give recitals and performances in Belfast. He also did some work in Dublin at the Theatre Royal.

While he was a spiritual and religious person, his sister, my Aunt Gabrielle, was very devout. She had great devotion to Our Lady. She had been at Ardboe, in County Tyrone, when Our Lady was said to have appeared there in 1954. She was reputed, while there, to have seen Our Lady's cloak trailing along the ground. She also had devotion to Our Lady of the Hill after an apparition was said to have occurred up near Castlewellan, again in 1954.

My dad and his sister headed off by getting the ferry to England and then working their way downwards to Dover. They eventually got the train from France to Italy and then made their way from Rome to Foggia and on to San Giovanni. It would have been a tough trip at the time, not long after the war.

Apparently, in Rome, my aunt was trying to ask one of the local policemen for directions to the bus. He started to get agitated. She took out her powder puff and was puffing her face, trying to keep his attention. Unfortunately, the powder went all over his uniform. Dad said he just wanted to climb down a drain!

When they got to San Giovanni, they stayed in the only hotel that was there at the time. Dad's musical ability soon came to people's attention. At dinner, one day, he was given a piano-keyed accordion and was asked to play a couple of tunes. He did this and it seems they liked it. Afterwards, every time he would come into the restaurant the Italian owners would say, 'The musical maestro!'

Eventually, my dad received Holy Communion from Padre Pio. The occasion is recorded in a black-and-white photo. You can see Dad in a heavy coat and wearing a scarf and a white shirt, with dark, neat hair and with his mouth open, receiving the communion on his tongue. In the photo, Padre Pio is distributing it with his right hand and you can make out the mitten quite clearly.

Gabrielle is kneeling on Dad's left. She is wearing a hat with a veil and is looking very devout. There is an extraordinary look of love on her face. However, the centrepiece of the photo is Padre Pio, who looks very peaceful and compassionate. We still have the photo to this day.

My dad also went to confession with Padre Pio. He was given a sheet with a list of misdemeanours or sins on it and he had to tick off what applied to him. This was apparently because Padre Pio didn't speak English, although he understood it. When he was in confession, the padre listened intently to him and then gave him a sort of a tap on the jaw. It was a light, gentle tap, probably implying, 'You bold boy!'

My Aunt Gabrielle also went to confession with him. She

said that he was harder on the women than on the men. In addition, Dad had his hands blessed by Padre Pio. He really had a remarkable touch with his hands and they had meant a lot to him. He was, after all, a concert pianist and he taught piano as well. The blessing must have pleased him a lot.

After they came back, Padre Pio continued to play a role in our family. I remember my mother got bowel cancer in 1973. I was only five years old at the time. Our grandmother got a Padre Pio mitten to have her blessed with it. She had to jump through a few hoops to get it. Unfortunately, Mum died from the cancer, aged 49, and my dad was knocked for six.

When I got older, I also developed devotion to Padre Pio. In my teens, I had gone away from the church, but I eventually came back and I began to pray to him. I then decided I should go to San Giovanni, probably to make the same journey my dad had made. I felt drawn to where he had gone and also to Padre Pio. It was just something I wanted to do.

I suppose that I wanted the next generation to maintain the connection between our family and Padre Pio. I wanted to confirm our link with his narrative and his mysticism and his intense holiness. But it was also partly for me. I had this sense that he was a very holy man and I wanted to be around where he was and to get the feeling of having been there.

Unfortunately, that time, I never saw Padre Pio's body. On the day I arrived, they had closed the place where he was to go on display, in order to do renovations. I also went back in 2011, for a second pilgrimage, and I didn't see the body then either because it was no longer on view; it had been reinterred in a sealed casket. So, unlike my dad, I never saw Padre Pio.

On that second trip, my brother Patrick accompanied me. He is also a concert pianist, just like my dad was. When we were there, in our hotel, some of the pilgrims we were with knew of his musical talent. They asked him if he would play the piano for them. That's what he did. He gave an impromptu recital in the lounge of the hotel, to the delight of the pilgrims and hotel staff. It was reminiscent of what had happened with my father all those years before.

I was a bit disappointed that I never saw Padre Pio, but maybe he had a reason why that should have been. However, my dad's visit is still recalled in our family. We talk about it when we're together. It might come up in conversation. On those occasions, we remember how my dad and my aunt made their pilgrimage to San Giovanni to see Padre Pio over half a century ago.

Kay Delamere, from County Offaly, met Padre Pio in San Giovanni in 1967.

John and I got married in September 1967and we went to Rome on honeymoon. We spent a few days in Rome and then we went down to San Giovanni to see Padre Pio. I knew a lot about his life at the time. My eldest sister was Mairead Doyle and she was the person who really brought devotion to Padre Pio to Ireland. She had gone to visit him many times in the 1950s, when it was very tough to get there, and she told us all about him.

Mairead organised talks and films about Padre Pio all over Ireland, including at the Gresham Hotel in Dublin. She really had great faith in him. Every time she'd come back from San Giovanni, we'd ask her about what had happened and what he was like. She'd tell us how lovely and holy he was. She would also tell us how he could see into other people's souls.

As a result, she got the five girls and the boy in our family to work for him and we all got involved.

During our visit back in 1967, we met Padre Pio as he was on the way into the church. A friend of mine, who was a priest, brought us over to him and he explained in Italian who we were. He told him we had just got married. Padre Pio put his arm around my shoulder and he said, 'God bless you and the children that you will have.' He said it in Italian, but the priest we were with translated it for us.

He was so natural doing it. He was really approachable and relaxed. You didn't come away from him thinking, 'Oh, he's so holy!' He also listened to you and, no matter how big a crowd that was there, you always felt he was looking at you. I remember he looked like any man in his 60s, with his grey hair going a bit scarce on top and with a beard. He was dressed in his habit and he had mittens on his hands.

We also saw him saying Mass during our visit. We went in the very early morning, which was more like the middle of the night. We got up at four or five o'clock. The Mass was special. He concentrated on what he was doing and everybody else concentrated with him. Everyone listened intently to what he was saying, although we were also trying to see his hands.

After Mass, we went to the sacristy to meet him. He spoke to all of us in Italian and he also blessed us all. We were all mesmerised. When he blessed you, he wasn't just doing it for the sake of it. We realised that he was genuinely holy and that he really meant what he was doing.

I never met him alive again. He died the following year, in 1968. Two of my sisters were in Rome at the time and they went to the funeral. However, I already had my first baby, so I couldn't go. Within a few years, I had two more and all three of them were born through Caesarean section. I then gave my cots and my prams and other stuff away and I said, 'That's it.' However, seven-and-a-half years later, I had Neil, the comedian, and I christened him Neil Pio.

I've gone to San Giovanni every year, at the end of October, since my kids got bigger. The only time I didn't go was when they were very small. Every time I'd travel there, I would go to see Padre Pio's coffin. I was also in Rome for his canonisation, after which we travelled on to San Giovanni.

The first night we were in San Giovanni, on that visit, my sister Mairead became very ill. We were staying in the same hotel. We were downstairs, having a cuppa, while she was in her room. I remember a priest came down for us and we all rushed upstairs. I held her hands and said the Rosary, while she got the last rites. She was then moved to the hospital and she passed away. It seemed appropriate that she died in San Giovanni. She is buried in Dublin, alongside my mother and father.

To this day, I am devoted to Padre Pio. All my children are, too, including Neil. Padre Pio was such a holy man, but he was also an ordinary individual, an ordinary 'Joe Soap'. He was great with people and very good to them. Yet, when you were talking to him, you could also see that he was different. He would always listen to you, even if he didn't understand what you were saying. He was interested in everybody. You also knew he belonged to God and he believed in what he was doing. He was certainly sincere; that's the best word for him.

MILLIE, FROM COUNTY MEATH, who has received lifelong support from Padre Pio, has been devoted to him since the 1960s.

I left for England in 1948 and trained there as a nurse. I then came back to Ireland in the early 1950s, but I eventually met my husband and we decided to return to England around 1955. We lived there in rented accommodation, but we hoped to have our own house. It took until the early 1960s before we could really afford to buy one. By then, I had three children and was expecting another.

We were living in digs at the time. We needed a deposit, but we didn't have it. I tried to borrow the money from three people, who were friends and relatives, but I couldn't get it and I feared that we would lose out on the house. However, I was great at praying and I asked Padre Pio and St. Jude for help.

Even at that stage, I absolutely loved Padre Pio. I had an aunt who was a nun and she was always giving us pictures and prayers and I think she had given me one of Padre Pio. She told me, 'He's a very good man.' I liked the look of him and I liked the prayer, too, because it was short. There was really something different about him, including the stigmata. I think I fell in love with him.

Around that time, I had to go into hospital for a bladder operation, which wasn't serious, and an old lady was in the bed beside me. She was a nice person and we got on very well. I used to bring her a bowl of water in the morning to save her from having to go into the bathroom to wash. I remember she loved *Songs of Praise*, which was on TV at the time.

One Sunday evening, after we had been released from the hospital, she came to visit and asked, 'How's the house purchase going?' I told her my story and said that we couldn't get the deposit and we might lose the house. Later, my husband was taking her home and she asked him if he would bring her to the bank on the following morning. He said, 'Of course.'

The next day, he brought her to the bank. When she came out, she handed my husband an envelope and said, 'I want you to pass that on to Millie.' He thought it was a letter or something. When I opened it, there was £300 inside. I was gobsmacked. It was meant as a gift, but I eventually paid it back. I believe Padre Pio and St. Jude got us that house.

Padre Pio, of course, was alive at that time and was living in San Giovanni. I was so thankful for what he and St. Jude had done. I prayed to him all the time or at least as much as I could. I sometimes neglected him, especially when I ended up with six children and I wouldn't have time to say a Hail Mary. However, I never forgot how he helped us.

After that, I followed him always. I remember watching news of his death on TV. That was in 1968. I was quite enthralled with what was happening. I was also sad that I had never gone on a pilgrimage to San Giovanni to see him when he was alive. It was one of my biggest regrets.

My husband died in 1989 and I then returned to Ireland in the late 1990s. I was back here for about 14 years when I got awful pains in my shoulders and arms. The pain was very severe. It was nagging away all the time. It really got me down and I could hardly eat or sleep. It made me very ill.

I went to the doctor and he said it was arthritis. He put me on tablets, but they were no good; the effects would last only half an hour. He then said, 'Would you try morphine patches?' I said, 'I would try anything to get rid of the pain.' So I tried morphine patches.

Eventually, I got a pain in my chest and I was rushed to hospital. I was very poorly. They sent for my children and told them that I was quite ill. On the second evening, a man came in with the Padre Pio glove. He blessed me with it and put it in my hand. He said prayers, too. He came in every night after that, for the seven nights I was in hospital.

On one of those nights, I had a vision of Padre Pio. He came to me in a dream and he was younger than he was when he died. He was dressed in his friar's clothes. There was a young priest with him, who I didn't know. There was another young person with him, who I didn't know either. All three of them appeared while I was in my bed, sometime after 12 o'clock at night.

Padre Pio came up to me and he said, 'We're going to San Giovanni.' He took me by the hand and he brought me there. We went to the church and knelt there and prayed for what I felt was the whole night. Padre Pio was on the outside of the seat, with me beside him and the young priest was on the other side of me. The young fellow, who was about 18 or 19 years of age, was on the inside.

We said the Padre Pio prayer and the Hail Mary and the Our Father. We then had a long time in silence. Padre Pio would only pray a bit, but I prayed even through the silence. It all came to an end when I woke up. I felt very much at peace and a lot better. I said, 'Thank you, St. Pio.' My son, who was there at the time, said, 'You're talking to yourself.' I said, 'No, I'm not. I'm talking to Padre Pio.'

Later, the man who brought the Padre Pio glove showed me a photograph of the church in San Giovanni and it was the very same church I saw that night. The moment he showed it to me, I said, 'That's the church I was in!' I had never seen it before.

I improved and improved and improved after that. The doctor took me off the morphine and all the other tablets I was taking. I started to eat and feel better again. Each time I ate before that, I would be so sick and bring the food up. But there was no more sickness and I enjoyed my food once more. I also have no more pain; only a bit of stiffness.

I attribute everything to Padre Pio. I firmly believe he was the person who helped me. I think that he has great powers; I cannot even express in words what I think of them. He is a wonderful saint and he means everything to me. He is always with me and always by my side. No matter what happens, he'll help me and I'll be well. He's definitely my number one saint.

COLETTE, FROM COUNTY KILKENNY, is also a long-standing devotee of Padre Pio. Her devotion to him began in the late 1960s, just before his death.

My interest in Padre Pio began when I was 14 years of age. My aunt was a nun in America and she sent home two books for us to read. One was about the life of Padre Pio; the other was about Sister Faustina. I hadn't heard of Padre Pio up to then, but I read the book and, even though it was a little bit advanced for me, I developed a love for him that never went away.

What I learned from the book had such an effect on me that, for three months, I would walk around the fields contemplating how one person could have such an impact on so many other people. His understanding of other people and his love for Jesus appealed to me. He was such a humble man. I felt Jesus had picked him to bring people back to what his passion was all about.

I got hooked on him and he became my best friend and my whole life. Since then, he has come first in everything I do. I grew up, left school and went to work, but I always had this love for him. I constantly placed my family under his protection. I talked to him constantly and told him how I felt, bad or good. I always put my trust in him and I told other people to do so, too.

I eventually got married and my young lad got sick. He was three years of age and I was expecting my second child at the time. He had an infection in his leg, on the bone, which they thought was cancerous. They were taking him in for an operation, but he got pneumonia and they couldn't operate. They had to let the pneumonia clear up and he was waiting in the hospital for ages.

I went in to visit him, one day, and he said, 'A priest came to visit me.' I asked him, 'Was it our priest?' He said, 'No, it was a priest with a beard, he had a long robe on him, and he told me I'm going to be alright.' I couldn't understand it as I hadn't been in contact with any friars. There was really nobody it could have been.

One Sunday night, while still waiting for the operation, I got a phone call telling me that my son was being operated on the following day. I went in on the Monday and the doctor called me aside. He said, 'I thought that before the operation I would do another X-ray on your son's leg. When I did, there was no sign of infection or anything else. It's cleared up completely. I don't know where it went, but it's gone.' My son was released from hospital and he was allowed home.

In the meantime, someone had given to my mother a little

picture of a young Padre Pio. It was up on a shelf in the kitchen. I stopped off at her house on the way home. My son sat on her lap and looked up at the shelf. He said, 'There's the man that came to see me! He's the man who told me I was going to get better!' I knew immediately what had happened. I said to Mammy, 'Now we know!' I believe it was Padre Pio brought me a miracle.

Unfortunately, I lost my second child. She died five minutes after being born and the doctors couldn't provide any reason why. We christened her Mary, after the mother of God. I was heartbroken, but I always believe Padre Pio wanted her and she went straight to God. However, I was left with my first child, who was saved.

My belief in Padre Pio developed after that. I continued to pray to him, although I have a funny way of doing it. I talk to him. I say, 'I know you loved the Rosary, but I haven't got the same way of saying it as you.' So, while I do say the Rosary, I tell him about everything that's going on. I think that's what he wants people to do. If you read about him, it's not just about praying; it's about looking at your own soul and trying to lead a better life.

Lots of different things happened to me after that. I lost another baby, but I became pregnant again. Unfortunately, I was in hospital for about six months of the pregnancy. The child wasn't growing and the doctors told me that it mightn't survive. They were afraid of a concealed haemorrhage. I left everything in the hands of Padre Pio. I said to everyone, 'This child will be born well. I know it.' My son was eventually born in perfect health and I know Padre Pio had a role in that.

The time came when he was three years of age and my mother, who was 80, was dying of a weak heart. I was at work and my sister was minding the two of them. My son had a fierce fascination for cutting newspapers into shapes; there weren't many toys around in those times. He had been up in the bed with Mammy, cutting the newspapers, when he came down to my sister. 'Come up quickly,' he said. 'Padre Pio is with Nanny in the room.'

My sister went up and all she could get was the smell of roses. She said it was the most beautiful scent and it was only in the bedroom. My mother died about five weeks later and I have no doubt Padre Pio had been with her.

The Sunday after she died, I got the smell again. I was at Mass and I went into the seat she always went into. There was nobody else there for five seats in front of me and ten seats behind. Yet I got the most beautiful smell of roses. I looked around and the nearest person to me was about ten to 12 feet away; it was a man and it wasn't coming from him. I think it was Padre Pio telling me she was with him.

Another remarkable thing happened around the time of his canonisation. I was at home when I heard about it on the radio. I found out that a trip was going to Rome, but it cost €1,129 and I couldn't afford it. I said to Padre Pio, 'If you want me to go, please help me get the money.' Soon afterwards, a letter came from Irish Life to my husband enclosing a cheque on a life policy he had taken out on his mother, who had died. The cheque was for €1,129. My husband gave it to me and I went to Rome.

There have been loads of events. I recently went to the Holy Land and an extraordinary thing occurred. I was in Ephesus looking at Our Lady's house. I was talking aloud to Our Lady and saying to her, 'I never got to see St. Pio this year.' A man beside me heard me and he said, 'He came to see you.' I turned around and it was Fr. Ermelindo, who had looked after Padre Pio in San Giovanni for three years before he died. Things happen with Padre Pio big time.

I really feel he is my guardian angel. He's in my heart. He's been that way since I was 14 and I'm 59 now. He's been with me in bad times and good times. Since I first read about him, I have never gone to sleep once without praying to him. I pray to him every day of the week. I don't only pray during the good times; if you don't do it during the bad times, too, then you really have no faith.

Most importantly, though, I talk to him. I have a beautiful statue of him on the stairs and, when I go upstairs, I say hello to him and I feel a sort of warmth coming back from him. A statue of Our Lady is beside his and I tip her, too. But, above all, I tell Padre Pio about everything that happens in my life, good and bad. I think that's what he likes. After that, I leave everything in his hands and he always helps me.

KATHLEEN, FROM COUNTY KERRY, traces her devotion to a dream she had of Padre Pio more than half a century ago.

My first experience of Padre Pio happened in the early 1960s, when he was still alive. I had no real connection with him at that stage. I never prayed to him or anything like that, although I would have known about him and heard about him through prayer leaflets. However, on that occasion, in the early 1960s, he appeared to me in a dream. I recognised him immediately through his Capuchin friar's habit and his grey beard.

In the dream, he was carrying a handmade, low-down stool, made of wicker. He handed me the stool and then said, 'Sit down there and I'll hear your confession.' When I woke up the following morning, I said, 'That was Padre Pio and he came to hear my confession! What have I done wrong? What have I neglected to do? What sin did I commit? Did I omit to tell something in confession?' I was worried a bit for a while.

That dream was the first time Padre Pio impacted on my life. I then started reading all about him and found out that confession was one of the things dearest to his heart. He spent hours upon hours in the confession box. I suppose that what happened helped me to look into my own way of going to confession and my examination of conscience. I took a big interest in him after that.

He eventually became a great example to me of how I should deal with suffering. He taught me that through the cross we could obtain salvation. On one occasion, Jesus asked him, 'Would you have abandoned me if I had not crucified you? Beneath the cross one learns to love and I do not grant this to everyone but only to those souls who are dearest to me.' Padre Pio suffered all the time and he learned to love. I have had my share of crosses, too, and while I am not anxious to suffer, Padre Pio taught me to embrace it.

He taught me that suffering is given to most people and we should use it well. He was a tremendous example of how to deal with it in a positive way. I saw pictures of him saying Mass towards the end and he was really in pain. Instead of becoming bitter, as many people do, it can be used positively. It can teach people how to love. It's also a great resource for redeeming souls. I often tell people who are suffering, perhaps from illness or handicap, 'Don't forget to offer it up and you will redeem a lot of souls.'

A short time before his death, I wrote him a letter and sent

Early Years

it to San Giovanni Rotondo. This was around 1965 or 1966. I asked him for his prayers for my intentions. The letter that I received back read: 'Padre Pio sends you his blessing and will pray for your intentions. He urges you to have complete trust in the goodness of God and to pray always according to his divine will. Padre Pio thanks you for your offering.'

The letter was signed by the Fr. Superior as I think Padre Pio wasn't well at that stage. I still have it, with the stamp of San Giovanni in the corner. It is faded and a bit tattered, but I treasure it. I don't read it often, yet it is lovely to have.

I also became a 'spiritual daughter' of Padre Pio. I enrolled, at the time, with San Giovanni. It was just something you did and you had your name included. He promised that he would wait inside the gates of paradise until all of his children are safely home. It means a lot to me.

My youngest son was similarly attracted to Padre Pio. They share the same birthday: 25 May. He was only 11 years of age at the time of my husband's death. He told me that he was confused about it and he couldn't understand how a person could die from natural causes; he thought his father must have died in an accident.

But my son discovered a prayer to Padre Pio in my father's pocket and for six months afterwards he prayed only to him; he didn't pray to anyone else. Today, that same son is doing great work with teenagers. I think his compassion might have something to do with Padre Pio, although who can say?

Looking back, I think there were many reasons why I was drawn to Padre Pio. I suppose, like Mother Teresa and Pope John Paul II, we were living with a saint in their own time. From that point of view, he was real to us. He was also the first stigmatised priest; St. Francis was stigmatised, but he wasn't a priest. In addition, he read minds and was severe with people who were not upfront with the truth. He was also silenced at one stage and straight away he obeyed. He was a great example of everything to do with the church.

He was also very paternalistic and, in that sense, there was something of my own father in him. Because of that, I can talk to him. I have a lovely picture of him hanging in my hallway. I sometimes stop, when I pass it, and say a prayer to him or tell him about something that is going wrong and ask him to help me.

He was clearly chosen for a special role, with his whole life dedicated to relieving the physical and spiritual suffering of everybody else. He welcomed his own suffering. He was one of the few people I know of who did that. He had the five wounds of Christ on his body and was continually in pain. In that way, he put a great meaning on what suffering could be used for. If people could view their suffering in the way he did, it would make it all the more positive, wouldn't it?

MICHAEL, FROM COUNTY LIMERICK, outlines Padre Pio's role in his daughter's recovery from cancer. His awareness of Padre Pio first arose in the very late 1960s or early 1970s.

Some years ago, my relationship with God was like a phone conversation on a bad line; it wasn't totally lost, but it was very poor. Eventually, I started going to different prayer meetings and prayer groups and I got reconnected with my faith. One of them was a prayer group where a man called Donald Enright used to speak. He was a big devotee of Padre Pio and he would describe healings and things like that.

I had, of course, known of Padre Pio from an earlier age. My grandmother and grandfather had been to San Giovanni back in the 1950s. I remember, as a young child, in the late 1960s or early 1970s, they told me about being there. My grandmother went to confession to him and found him to be very strict. She told me about the stigmata. She said he was a 'cross' man, although she believed in him and she was very devout. Donald Enright had met him, too, and he likewise believed in him.

I remember Donald told one particular story about someone who got cancer and had a reprieve through Padre Pio. Donald pointed out that, although the cancer did come back and the person died, the grace the person got was an acceptance facing death. He felt that came through Padre Pio. He told us lots of other stories about people who were at death's door, or beyond hope, and they got healings.

Initially, I was sceptical. I think it's in our nature to be that way. However, the meetings incited an interest in me and I started reading literature about Padre Pio. I wanted to find out more about him and I read maybe four or five books. I read about people who had witnessed his bilocation and about people who described how he had come to them or had other supernatural experiences of him. I also read about his meeting with Karol Wojtyla, the future Pope John Paul II, and it impressed me. I got really caught up in the whole thing.

I also read about the doubts: that Padre Pio would use stuff on his hands to cause the stigmata and that he would use perfume. On a ratio of about ten to one, I ended up feeling that there was definitely something to the man. I'm reluctant to say that any person has special powers. In fact, Padre Pio always stated that he was only the channel and that it was Jesus was the healer; he intercedes and the healing only comes through him. That's the way I look at it, too. But I definitely think there was something special to Padre Pio.

A few years ago, my young daughter became unwell. One weekend, she became very sluggish and wasn't getting out of bed. Her skin looked strange. A doctor thought she might have meningitis. She was admitted to hospital and we were waiting ages for results. Eventually, the results came back and they showed that she had leukaemia.

We were absolutely shocked. My own mother was dying of cancer at the time and I remember thinking, 'God, how could you do this to me, with my mother and daughter both having cancer!' I felt I was going to explode. I felt like there was petrol, or high-octane fuel, running through my veins. Every part of my body was working overtime. It was like I was spring-loaded. I can't describe it any other way.

My daughter was admitted to hospital for treatment. She got chemotherapy and they were very confident they could get on top of it. Unfortunately, as time went on, complications arose. She had to get platelet transfusions and, on one occasion, she had an allergic reaction which nearly killed her. All her glands swelled up and she almost died that night.

Overall, she nearly died four times. She also got an infection, as a side-effect from her chemo, which caused a growth in her head. It wasn't a tumour, but it had the same texture as one and was affecting her brain. She had to be operated on and we thought she was finished. She was in a bad way.

At one stage, about a month or a month-and-a-half after she was diagnosed, I got a Padre Pio mitt in to her. We put it in the bedside locker beside her and it was there with her for a few nights. We also prayed a lot. I prayed to God and I prayed to Padre Pio to intercede. When I prayed, I definitely meant it because I did not want to see my daughter suffer. I remember saying, when I was giving the glove back, 'I hope this does something.'

Although a lot of bad stuff happened after that, she eventually improved a lot. Things started coming around and she started responding. Things started to come right. She then gradually got better. We had been expecting the worst and that she was going to die. But, ever since then, she has never looked back. She is fine to this day.

I believe in divine intervention and I believe Padre Pio helped, although I believe he is only the conduit and not the healer. To think otherwise would be to equate him with God, which would be wrong. He cannot be equated with God. The 'higher power' is God; it is important to say that and believe that. All you can do is to ask Padre Pio to intercede for you and he certainly has a very special connection with God.

I certainly think, in the case of my daughter, that he had a role to play. I know, at the time, we tried everything. A lot of people prayed to so many saints for their help, so I tend to look on what happened as a collective. But that my daughter is alive is a miracle. I believe Padre Pio and getting the glove and all the praying I did caused that miracle and got her well.

PAT, FROM COUNTY OFFALY, recalls Padre Pio's involvement in his child's recovery from pneumonia in the 1970s.

My son developed double pneumonia in 1973. He was only five weeks old, a lovely brown-eyed boy and our first child. He became very chesty and bronchial. He also had a high fever. We were worried, especially because it was late January and the weather was very bad. There was a lot of heavy snow on the ground and we couldn't get him to the hospital. The roads were impassable and we were trapped. We had to deal with the problem at home.

Our local doctor used to come to treat him. He lived quite near us, so he came three times a day to give our son an injection. On one occasion, he arrived at 3.30 in the morning. I think that surprised us, as we didn't know how ill Paul was. I think the doctor had realised that the child was deteriorating. It was then that he told us there was a possibility we could lose him. We were shocked and panic set in.

At the time, my mother had great devotion to Padre Pio. She had been a devotee of his since he was alive and he was always part of our household. She had medals, which somebody had brought back from San Giovanni. She had a picture of him up in her bedroom. She had even been over to San Giovanni on a pilgrimage.

I was in my mid-20s and didn't have any devotion to him myself. I would have heard him mentioned in the house, but I also heard of other saints like St. Anthony. All I knew was that he was a priest in the south of Italy and that he had the wounds of Jesus. While I went to Mass and said my prayers, an interest in Padre Pio hadn't rubbed off on me yet.

My mother was very worried about Paul. She had access to one of Padre Pio's mittens and she went and got it. The woman she borrowed it from had been to San Giovanni and had met Padre Pio. She had great devotion to him. Early in the morning, my mother brought the glove to us and, if I remember correctly, she was there with my father along with me and my wife.

The glove was placed on Paul's chest and a prayer was said asking for Padre Pio's intercession. We promised that if he was cured, and if we had a second child, we would name that child in honour of Padre Pio. To be truthful, I didn't know

Early Years

what to expect. It was a time of crisis and I was grasping at all kinds of straws. Although I didn't believe in miracles at the time, I would try anything for my child.

From the time the glove was put on Paul's chest, he started to improve. He had been lifeless, but he started to become a lot more active in his cot. He began to take notice of us and everything around him. His temperature came down and he started to come back to life. He soon returned to his normal self.

I am certain that the turning point was when the glove arrived. It was only after he was blessed with the glove that he started to improve and I have no doubt that he only got well through the intercession of Padre Pio. My mother believed that, too, and she shed tears of relief and joy. We also kept our promise and we named our next child, a little baby girl, Pia.

My devotion to Padre Pio began immediately. What happened changed my life. I had never bothered with the Padre Pio pilgrimages to Holy Cross Abbey and to Knock, which my mother used to organise at that time, but from then on I got involved with helping her. I promised her before she died in 1997 that I would bring groups to San Giovanni and I have done it every year since 1999.

I have also got the scent of roses. I first got it at Padre Pio's tomb in San Giovanni. It was overwhelming. I got it for a few seconds and then it went away. I looked around to see if someone was there wearing perfume, but no one was. I have got that same aroma many times since, including in my house. I know it's regarded as the smell of roses, but if you were to smell roses from now until the day you die, you would never get the real aroma of Padre Pio.

I believe I saw a miracle happen with my son. I don't think

Paul would have improved without Padre Pio's help; instead, I believe he would have died. I've seen Padre Pio answer so many requests, including the case of a woman who had a very large tumour whose cancer disappeared and another lady who had cancer for nine years but who is now completely clear. So Padre Pio is genuinely a powerful saint. Looking at what happened with my son, I have absolutely no doubt of that whatsoever.

ANN, FROM COUNTY LOUTH, reflects on her baby daughter's miraculous cure.

My story dates back to 5 December 1975, when I was about to give birth to my baby daughter. Her heartbeat was so rapid before she was born that they thought I was having twins, but an X-ray showed that wasn't so. They decided to induce her. The moment they started to do so, her heart began failing. They had to rush me down for an emergency Caesarean section.

The next thing I remember was that they were trying to wake me to tell me that the baby was gravely ill and they needed to christen her. I immediately knew things were bad. I remember thinking, 'If I keep my eyes closed and don't wake up, I won't have to face this or deal with it.' I was hoping it would all go away.

After I came around, the doctor said to me that I had given birth to a very ill baby and she wasn't going to live. I was told that I couldn't see her because of her grave condition. I also remember the doctor telling me to forget about the baby; there was something very seriously wrong with her heart. They then moved her to another hospital, while I stayed where I was.

The next morning, the consultant came to see me and my husband Jim. She told us that our daughter had been born

Early Years

with a malformed heart, had only three chambers instead of four, had a single ventricle and her liver was grossly enlarged. We were told that she was comfortable in an incubator and on medication to keep her heart beating. The consultant also said that her prospects were poor; she wasn't expected to live and nothing could be done.

I hadn't seen my baby at this stage, although my husband had. He told me that in the special-care nursery in the other hospital there were all these incubators around. The babies in them were deformed, or in a bad way, and he was saying to the doctors, 'Oh, my God! Look at that poor little thing.' When he came to our baby, she seemed to be perfectly normal. However, the doctor said, 'All those other babies have at least a one per cent chance of surviving, but I'm afraid your child doesn't have any.'

They eventually brought me by ambulance to see Kelly. They took her out of the incubator and that was the first time I held her. I remember, as I did, I tried to pass the life that was in me into her. I was saying, 'Hold on! I need to get to know you better!' I wanted her to know that I was her mammy; that seemed to be enough at the time.

A short while later, coming up to Christmas, I was told by one of the doctors that they had made a decision and that she was well enough for us to take her home. I thought, 'This is it. This is my chance to get her home and we'll be a little family at last.' The nurses were in tears when we were carrying her out on Christmas Day. However, the doctor who gave me her medication and her prescriptions reiterated, 'Your baby isn't going to live.'

It was around this time that Padre Pio first came into the picture. One night, my mother handed me a relic on a little prayer card and said, 'Pray to this man.' I said, 'Who is he?' She said, 'That's Padre Pio. He had the stigmata of Jesus.' She then said, 'He was a wonderful man. He could look into your soul and see what sort of person you are.' A sort of coldness overwhelmed me. I thought, 'I know I need a miracle, but if he looks into my soul, sinner that I am, he's not going to do anything for me.'

I handed the relic back to my mother. 'But I've been praying to him the whole way through your pregnancy,' she said. I replied, 'Well, keep doing so, because I won't. I'll keep praying to Our Lady and all the other saints, but not to him.' That's who I had been praying to all along. It was almost like I took an immediate dislike to Padre Pio.

After that, we went back for our monthly check-ups and they'd say, 'She's doing OK, but the prognosis is still the same. There's no change.' We were told that the longest a child had survived with Kelly's condition was four years. They said she would eventually outgrow her heart and she would probably just drift away in her sleep. We knew that coming up to four years was crucial.

Not too long before Kelly's fourth birthday, Padre Pio came back into the picture. It was just before she was due to go to hospital for a big test to see how things were. A person said to me, 'Did you ever think of getting Kelly blessed with the glove of Padre Pio?' I said, 'What glove?' She told me about a woman who had a glove and that her brother, who had been unwell, was blessed with it and he was fine.

On the Sunday, the day before Kelly was due in hospital for the test, we drove to see the woman. I didn't even know her name. While I knew the town where she lived, I didn't know where her house was. When we arrived, I asked a man, 'Where does the woman who has the Padre Pio glove live?' He said, 'You're parked just outside her door!' I took Kelly in to see the lady and she took out this glove and blessed her with it.

The woman also gave me a Padre Pio prayer leaflet and that night was the very first time that I prayed to him. About 20 minutes after finishing the prayer, Kelly was standing next to the side of my bed. She said, 'Mammy, you've got to come in, there's an old man in my room.' I said, 'Kelly, there's no one there.' I thought she was dreaming or had a temperature.

I brought her back to her room and tucked her into bed. As I did so, she looked over my shoulder and pointed into the corner and she said, 'Look, Mammy, he's smiling at me!' I said, 'There's no one there.' Padre Pio never even entered my head at that point. Later, as I fell asleep, I could hear Kelly giggling and having a conversation.

The next morning, as we were getting ready to leave for the hospital, I asked Kelly to go into the sitting-room and get my cigarettes out of my bag. After she went in, I heard her shouting, 'Mammy! Mammy!' and I rushed in. Kelly had seen some magazines that the woman with the glove had given me the day before. The front of one of them had this big picture of Padre Pio. 'Look, Mammy!' she said. 'That's him. That's the man who was in my room last night!'

We drove to the hospital straight after that. Her test was scheduled for the following day again. They were doing an angiogram. They took her down to theatre and my heart was breaking. About an hour later, they brought her back and she was deathly white. I asked the nurse, 'How did it go?' She said, 'The doctor will want to speak to you.'

We went in to see the doctor and he was sitting behind a desk. He said, 'I don't know how to explain this to you. For the last four years, you have been coming here with Kelly for tests and I haven't been able to give you any hope, because there wasn't any.

'Today, however, I have the tests that were done on Kelly at birth, which show that she had a congenitally abnormal heart, a single ventricle and a grossly-enlarged liver. I also have tests from today that show Kelly's heart is completely normal. Instead of one ventricle, she now has two and her liver is reduced in size.

'You can take her home, she's absolutely perfect. You've got a miracle and I don't know how you got it.' I said, 'I know exactly where I got it from!' After that, I rang everybody and told them what had happened. When I told my mother, she said, 'I told you that Padre Pio wouldn't let you down!'

Later, I went over to San Giovanni, where I spoke to Fr. Joseph. I asked him, 'Why did Padre Pio make me wait for four years?' He said, 'He didn't make you wait four years. You had to acknowledge him. You had to ask him. He was always going to cure her because your mother had been praying to him since birth. But you are her mother and you eventually asked him.'

In San Giovanni, I also smelled the perfume of Padre Pio. Fr. Joseph brought both Kelly and I into Padre Pio's cell. As I came out, I passed the statue of Our Lady of Fatima and I got this beautiful aroma. I said to Fr. Joseph, 'I just got Padre Pio's perfume.' I asked him, 'Why there and why not in his cell?' He said, 'He's telling you that Our Lady brought you to him and you must never forget about her.'

The rest is history. Kelly is now perfect and married and she has three children of her own. She's had her crosses in life, but she has no heart problems whatsoever. She's a very caring person and there are no repercussions from the condition that she once had. Whenever anything happens, she always turns to Padre Pio and she always knows that he's there. He's the one constant in her life. He's also the one who brought her back to me and gave her life.

ALBERT, FROM DUBLIN, has witnessed or experienced many favours from Padre Pio. His devotion began in the 1970s.

I didn't have great devotion to Padre Pio, but my wife did. Her family had lived near Church Street in Dublin, where the Capuchins are, so I suppose they were bound to be devoted to him. Her brother was a great devotee, too, along with his wife. They had gone to see him in San Giovanni when he was alive. They would show us pictures and tell us what they had seen.

I eventually bought into it big time. It would have been in the mid-1970s. I started doing novenas to Padre Pio and I would read any books I could get. I would also go to prayer meetings once a month and I'd hear some beautiful talks. I would read the Padre Pio magazine. I was really taken by him. You couldn't ignore this wonderful, saintly man.

The first time my wife was helped by him was when she developed arthritis in her spine. Some days, I'd come home and she'd be crying. She'd say, 'I can't make the beds. I can't kneel down because, if I do, I can't get back up again.' She was attending hospital for years, but nothing worked.

We eventually went to a man in Wicklow, who had a relic of Padre Pio. He lived in a cottage and the walls were decorated with Padre Pio pictures. My wife told him what was wrong. He said, 'I went to see Padre Pio when I was a little boy and he told my father I'd have the gift of healing.' He then said to my wife,

'Just loosen your coat. I'm going to put my hand on your back, where the pain is.'

She did so and he said, 'Tell me when you feel something.' She immediately said, 'I can feel a burning heat in your hand and the pain is moving down my leg.' 'That's fine,' he said. 'It's going to take about a month for your pain to disappear, but it will go.' Soon after, the pain went and it never came back. We felt that was remarkable.

On another occasion, around 1983 or 1984, we were trying to purchase a house but had problems finding the money. We had no security and we didn't even have a deposit. We went to a Padre Pio meeting, where we met up with my wife's brother. He said, 'You need a miracle. Pray to Padre Pio and you'll get one. He will answer your prayers.' We prayed to Padre Pio and we kept going to the prayer meetings.

So many things happened following that. One person led to another and to another. There were telephone calls and meetings with people we didn't even know. The day before the signing, the money came through. My sister said, 'You really must know somebody up there!' Even the solicitor said afterwards, 'I have never come across a case like this. I don't know how you did it, but nobody would ever come across the money like you did.' I have no doubt it was due to the intervention of Padre Pio.

Another strange thing took place a little bit later. A friend asked if I would pray for a couple in Belfast, who weren't getting on too good and the husband had stopped going to Mass. I said we would do a nine-day novena to Padre Pio. Two weeks later, the woman said, 'A strange thing happened on the eighth day of your novena. That man was going to a talk at Queen's University. His car wouldn't start. He said, "I'll fix it." So he went out to fix it, but he couldn't.

'As a result, he got to the university too late for the talk. There was another talk just starting and he decided to go to that instead. It was about Padre Pio. Later, he came home and told his wife that he had heard a lovely story about a priest named Padre Pio and he said he was going to start going to Mass again.' It was a lovely thing to happen.

I also remember, around that time, a person who wanted to repay us for a favour we did for him said, 'I'm going to book you on a trip over to San Giovanni and I will pay the deposit.' When it came near the time to pay the remainder, we owed what was £1,100 in those days. We didn't have it, but one day I got a letter from the Revenue Commissioners. The letter said, 'We owe you £1,100.' It was exactly the same amount. So off we went to San Giovanni.

We started in Rome, where my wife fell. We didn't know it then, but she had badly fractured her ankle. She hobbled on. Eventually, when we got to San Giovanni, she got her ankle blessed by Fr. Alessio with the glove of Padre Pio and we then brought her to the hospital. Her ankle was very swollen. The doctor said, 'We'll strap you up the best we can. But, if possible, don't walk on it.' He then pointed out, 'It has two fractures.'

She went on to do all of the Stations of the Cross in San Giovanni and she felt that, while I was holding one of her arms, somebody else was holding her other arm. She felt it was Padre Pio. We left San Giovanni and went to other places, including Loreto, where we went to Our Lady's house. My wife was standing up or walking all the time. We also went to

Monte Cassino and Castel Gandolfo, which are hilly, and she walked there as well.

Eventually, we came home to Ireland. I said, 'We had best go to the hospital and get you checked out.' She said, 'I want to go shopping first.' We got the shopping done and then went to the hospital. The doctor said, 'Well, it can't be a fracture, because you couldn't have walked if you had one.' She said, 'But the doctor in San Giovanni said it was.'

They X-rayed her and they found two heavy fractures. The doctor, who was extremely surprised, said, 'The fractures are healing and they're healing very well.' They gave her crutches, which she never used, and four weeks later, when we went back, the doctor told her, 'Somebody up there must love you because your ankle is perfectly healed.' Here we were, on our first visit to San Giovanni, and Padre Pio had performed a miracle.

I still pray to Padre Pio, not as deeply as I did before because nowadays my greatest link is with the Blessed Virgin Mary. I'm very much into the Rosary now. It's a different path I'm on. But I have no doubt Padre Pio was leading me there as he had great devotion to Our Lady.

I think that he was a most wonderful, holy man. The stories regarding him are unbelievable, like the pilot coming over in a plane during the last war to bomb San Giovanni and he saw a monk in the sky, so he didn't bomb the town. Later, when that pilot visited San Giovanni, he recognised that the monk was Padre Pio.

There are other amazing stories about him in confession, where he would know things that people weren't telling him and he would tell them what they were leaving out. So I am awestruck by this holy man. He was very powerful.

Early Years

He was so committed to the Lord and he believed totally in the power of God. Because of that, I believe in him and I believe in the power of his prayer before the Lord. I have no doubt in my mind about him. He always said, 'Send me your guardian angel,' so I tell people who need something that that's what they should do. If you need something badly, he will get it for you.

MICHAEL, FROM COUNTY TIPPERARY, attributes his recovery from severe kidney problems to Padre Pio.

It all began in 1978, while I was living and working in Dublin. I was getting headaches and other little things like that. Later on, my feet started to swell. I went to hospital, where they did a biopsy and told me I had a bit of a kidney problem. They kept me in for a couple of weeks, but they never actually told me that my kidneys were failing. All I had to do was return for some check-ups.

Almost six years later, in early 1984, I began to feel very unwell. I was weak and tired. I would sit down at any time of the day and I'd fall into a deep sleep. Eventually, I had no appetite and wasn't able to eat. I found it very difficult to work and had to leave my job and return home. The doctors discovered that impurities had built up in my blood and my blood pressure was very high. I was actually coming to the end-stage of kidney failure.

I ended up back in hospital. This time, the consultant said, 'You're in a serious condition.' I was shocked. I knew I had a kidney problem, but nobody had actually said along the way, 'You're going to have kidney failure.' Maybe they would tell you more today. Perhaps I was young at the time and didn't ask. It all just crept up on me.

Things were very bad. My girlfriend, who is now my wife, called in to see me and spoke to the doctor. He said, 'If we can get him through the night, he'll live.' Things were that close; touch-and-go. They did a quick operation and put me on a kidney machine. I started to recover and was in hospital for about five or six weeks. I felt better and more energetic, although anything would have been an improvement on how I had felt beforehand.

One day, during my stay in hospital, I was walking around and I happened to sit down. A lady I had never seen before in my life sat down beside me. I remember it was a lovely spring day, in the month of April. She asked me, 'What's wrong with you?' We talked for a while. Before she departed, she handed me a little two-page booklet and said, 'This is a novena prayer to Padre Pio. You should say that.'

I knew very little about Padre Pio at the time. I knew about the wounds and other little things, but I hadn't been praying to him or anything like that. Given the situation I was in, and facing what I was facing, my reaction was, 'It certainly won't do me any harm.' So I took the booklet and that was the first time I ever prayed to Padre Pio.

I was on a kidney machine from then on and was up and down to Dublin. One day, around February or March of 1985, I was on my way up and was sharing the taxi with a lady. We started talking and she asked me how I was. I vaguely knew her. She said, 'Did you ever hear of Tom Cooney?' She was referring to the man in County Clare who had met Padre Pio and had relics of him. I said, 'No, I didn't.' She said, 'You should go to him, when you get a chance. He will bless you with the Padre Pio glove.'

At the time, the urea building up in my blood was so bad

Early Years

that I was itching very badly. I was scratching so much that I would bring the blood up in my skin. It was unbelievable, almost unbearable. It was so annoying that I said, 'I'm going to ring Tom Cooney.' I got an appointment for Good Friday 1985, around three o'clock. When I met him, I told him what was wrong and he blessed me with the glove and we briefly prayed together. The itch practically went after that. It was a lot more bearable. That was really the last day I had it.

Things improved in other ways, too. I was hoping I might be able to have a kidney transplant. They did tests on my family to see if one of my brothers or sisters would be suitable donors. My sister was home from Canada and they checked her out. I was pinning my hopes on her. Unfortunately, the doctor told me, 'I'm sorry, but I don't think she will be suitable.' I was devastated.

About a month later, I got a call to say, 'Your sister is suitable and they are going ahead with the operation.' They did the operation and my sister gave me one of her kidneys. I have hardly looked back since then. That was two positives: the stopping of the itching and the transplant. Although I really have no idea where all that came from, I know that the good luck followed my contact with Padre Pio.

My luck continued after that. I met with Tom Cooney, on another occasion, and he blessed me with a bit of cloth that Padre Pio used to wear on his hand, under his glove. He said, 'Anybody who is blessed with this will be lucky in life.' At the time, I had a job but was made redundant. A week later, I was back working again. The new company eventually went into liquidation, yet I was back working a month later. I have applied for other jobs but wasn't hired and was disappointed, yet it turned out, for various reasons, that I was blessed not to get them. Luck seemed to follow me.

I also experienced the perfume of Padre Pio. I have been to San Giovanni on a couple of occasions. On one of the trips, I was up at the Padre Pio statue, where they were saying the Rosary in the evening. I suddenly got this smell of roses. It was like the smell you would get in a rose garden. My wife got it as well. I walked away from where I was, thinking I might be smelling perfume from some of the ladies around me. But, no matter where I went, the smell followed me around.

I bought a booklet in San Giovanni and brought it home. My youngest girl, who was about ten or 11 at the time, was looking through it and said, 'There's a smell of flowers off the book.' My wife and I got no smell off it, but my daughter got it clearly. We think the aroma of Padre Pio followed us home.

Today, I am fine and living a normal life. I'm enjoying myself and my health is excellent. I still get my bloods checked every six months and they always turn out to be extremely good. I'm on tablets, which I still have to take because of the transplant. Otherwise, I'm absolutely 100 per cent. Unlike many of those who entered hospital with me in 1984 and who didn't make it through, I am very much alive.

I believe Padre Pio had a role in my recovery. I prayed to him and asked him to help me. I have looked to him for things and got them. I have had faith in him and I think you have to have that. Faith isn't that you ask for something today and it comes tomorrow. You ask once or twice and you don't keep asking.

I think prayer is important, too, although there isn't much point praying if you're going to go out and act crookedly the very next day or be unjust. I also believe that going to Mass is important and from a Church point of view I celebrate things like Christmas. I also celebrate Easter as well. It's not that you

Early Years

have to be intensely religious. You just allow Padre Pio into your life and pray to him and believe in him. That certainly has worked for me.

ANNE, FROM COUNTY CLARE, discovered that her daughter was very sick at an early age, but Padre Pio came to the rescue.

My daughter became ill about 40 years ago, when she was two-and-a-half. She developed a bad pain in her ankle and it became swollen. It was thought that she might have fallen, but I knew she hadn't. I noticed that, at night, she would be very hot. She also developed a sore throat. Eventually, a doctor said she would have to go to hospital. I became very worried.

Even though she was so young, she had always been very alert. She had been walking since 12 months, was able to speak perfectly since the age of a year-and-a-half and was very smart for her age. She was always that bit ahead. So it was a terrible shock to us and we didn't know what was going to happen. It was the last thing we expected.

She eventually went into hospital, where she was so sick. By this stage, both of her ankles had started to swell. We also felt that her head had gone to one side, with her head leaning towards her shoulder. The next thing, they diagnosed Still's disease, which would nowadays be called juvenile arthritis.

It was raging through her blood. They had to put splints on her legs and arms, just to keep her limbs straight while this thing raged through her body. They said, 'It could strike her lungs or heart and, if it does, that's it.' The doctor told us, 'She's a very sick child and in a critical condition.' They didn't hold out great hopes.

I had got to the stage where I couldn't even pray. I had

turned totally against God because the child was so unwell. There was no good news coming from anywhere and no one was expecting our daughter to pull through. I remember once asking a nurse, 'Is she suffering the same pain as an adult?' She said, 'She is.' I felt God wasn't being fair.

One day, my mother mentioned to me, 'Why don't you pray to Padre Pio?' She was a devotee of his and a very religious person. She was the sort of woman who would write away for all sorts of relics and she certainly wouldn't miss Mass even if she was dying. She had also told me stories about Padre Pio and had a picture of him hanging in our kitchen.

She told me, as well, about Tom Cooney, the Padre Pio devotee in County Clare who had relics and had met Padre Pio. I went to Tom and explained my daughter's story. He said he would visit her. She was about five months in the hospital, at this stage, and had become deformed. Her limbs were twisted and her body was like the body of a starving child from Biafra. Her teeth were protruding and she was in such pain. She was totally crippled and she would lie there with her mouth open, moaning.

Tom Cooney would go in to her every day at lunchtime. He would bless her with the mitten and other relics and pray to Padre Pio. She was still in great humour, even though she was in pain. He laughingly told me, on one occasion, that another child was screaming and she said, 'Tom, will you bless that baby. I have a headache from listening to him!' But I also remember once asking Tom, 'How is she, do you think?' He said, 'God gives and God takes, and we have to accept whatever happens.'

Tom visited her for about a month and we were going in, too. One day, while visiting, she said, 'There was a man at the

Early Years

window.' I said, 'Where?' 'Over there,' she said, pointing to a high-up window; this was a children's ward high up in the hospital. I asked her, 'What kind of man?' 'He had a long, white beard and a brown dress and a rope around his stomach. He just turned around and smiled,' she said. She was referring to Padre Pio and she will still tell you that to this day.

It wasn't long after that when the doctor called me aside and said, 'Your daughter is still seriously ill, but if she just goes home for a week or two, she might start eating and improve.' She was only 11-and-a-half pounds in weight and three years old. So we brought her home. I felt that was a turning point and it came not long after Tom Cooney's visits.

We eventually got her walking. She took little steps and, one day, I had to bring her to her doctor, so I put on her little shoes and walked in to him holding her little hand. He looked at her and didn't recognise her. I told him who she was. 'What!' he said. 'That child should never have walked.'

It took years from then on. She developed epilepsy and was going back and forth to the hospital. She had to be rushed to the hospital a couple of times, but she always fought back. What she needed was time and it was critical she reached the age of 13. She did reach 13 and, although she now has osteoarthritis, she is in her 40s. She hasn't been totally cured, but she has in many ways lived life to the full.

I took her to San Giovanni when she was 21. I had promised Padre Pio that I would do that. We saw the tomb and did everything else. I did the Stations of the Cross for her. We met Fr. Alessio and it was absolutely beautiful. We also went to Pietrelcina. She became a great believer in Padre Pio and Tom Cooney and she developed great faith.

She also smelled Padre Pio's 'perfume of roses' on many

occasions. She would come to me and tell me about it. I never got it, but she certainly did. I remember she would get it when I brought her home to my mother's house. As she grew up to be an adult, however, when she would get it she would have a fear that something was going to happen, but nothing ever did, thank God.

I also became so devoted to Padre Pio that it was like someone had lit a light inside of me. Around the time she first got sick, I hadn't been to confession for 12 months. One Saturday, I was in the church and praying to Padre Pio. I thought, 'I'd like to go to confession.' Back in those days, you had to wear a scarf on your head and I didn't have one. Another woman came up to me and said, 'I'll give you mine.' I couldn't be kept away from the church after that.

I continue to pray to Padre Pio. I have pictures of him up in my room and a relic in my pocket. I know my little girl was so ill that she couldn't have lived without him. If you put your faith and trust in him, he will hear you and be with you. I put my daughter in Padre Pio's hands and I think he looked at her and took pity on her. That was definitely what happened.

LIAM, FROM COUNTY TIPPERARY, recalls how Padre Pio helped him overcome a serious medical condition.

In 1979, I went for a job and got it, but I failed the medical. My medical showed a high level of protein in the urine. They didn't know what was causing it. They held the job open and advised me to get myself checked out. They said, 'If you're OK, we'll take you on; if not, then sorry.' That was the start of my problems.

I went to Dublin for my appointment with a consultant who, it turned out, was a cancer specialist. I felt absolutely

Early Years

fine at the time and I couldn't understand what was going on. I was working long days and that didn't bother me. I had great health and great energy. I was planning to get married to Margaret, my girlfriend.

The consultant said, 'We're going to have to book you in and check this out, sooner rather than later.' Everything seemed negative. On the way in to see him, we could see the hospital morgue. Some years before, a friend of Margaret's who was in his late teens had died from cancer while attending the same specialist. All the talk was negative. I felt I was coming to Dublin to die.

I was supposed to be in Dublin for two or three days of tests, but I ended up being there for almost six weeks. They did test after test after test. They did two or three kidney biopsies. They eventually said I had kidney disease and they had caught it at an early stage. I said, 'Thank God! This can be sorted out with tablets.'

They still kept me in. I was passing lots of blood clots, so I was afraid to go to the loo. My blood pressure was rising. I went downhill rapidly. I lost about two stone. I was losing so much weight, on a daily basis, that I'd go to the hospital shop and buy a packet of biscuits and eat them before I went to sleep, hoping it might put on a bit of weight.

The tests continued, week after week, and I was getting down. I felt, 'I'll never get home. I'll never get married. I'll end up in the morgue and they'll bring me back home in a box.' I prayed and prayed and prayed; prayer was about the only thing I could cling on to at the time.

Adding to the problem was that there were absolutely no mobile phones in those days and Margaret was in Tipperary. I wondered, 'Where is this going to lead? Am I ever going to get out of hospital?' Every time the doctors came in, at ten or 11 o'clock in the morning, all I wanted them to say was, 'You're going home.'

Towards the end of six weeks, I was lying in bed. It was a Tuesday, which I'll never forget. There were six people in the ward, two of whom were gone for tests, and it was around three o'clock in the afternoon. I was feeling very sorry for myself. Suddenly, this Franciscan came in, dressed in his flowing brown habit, and although it was March he wore sandals with no socks. He was a dark-haired man who wore glasses.

The Franciscan was looking for one of the men who had gone down for tests. He started chatting away and eventually asked, 'Would anyone like to be blessed?' I thought, 'It won't do any harm.' I put up my hand. He went around to the other three men and then came to me last, on his way out.

He came over, took out a relic of Padre Pio, sat on the edge of the bed, blessed me, said a prayer and started to leave. As he was about to go, he said, 'I'm going to leave you now. Your wishes may not come true, but this might help. God bless you.' All I said in my mind was, 'Just let me go home.'

He turned around and walked out the door. It wasn't even like he was walking; it was more like he was floating. It was probably because of the sway of the habit that he looked that way. I can still see how graceful he looked. He just swished through the door in an arch, turning to the right. It was a bit like seeing a lady at a dance, with a calf-length dress, swinging around.

The instant he did so, a doctor wearing a white coat walked in through the door. They must have touched shoulders as they passed. He came in, walked to my bed and said, 'Liam, you're going home.' Every time I think of it, I still feel goose pimples in my neck. It might seem a minor incident to a lot of people, but to me, after six weeks, it was a miracle, a gift from heaven.

I didn't even ask the doctor for an explanation. He didn't offer one either. I couldn't have cared less if he had told me I only had six months to live. The only other thing he asked me was, 'Have you any way of getting home?' I thought of someone, a friend of mine in Dublin, who could give me a lift to the train station, so I said, 'I have.' All I wanted to do was get out.

It was 22 years later before I really got sick again. Around 2001, I started to feel very tired. It was an unusual tiredness. One day, I went off into work and I just could not stand. I couldn't understand what was wrong with me. I was sent back up to Dublin, where I was told, 'Things are starting to deteriorate.' They told me I'd have to go on dialysis, which I dreaded.

I said a few prayers again to the good man. All I wanted to do was stay away from hospitals, operations and doctors. I'd had enough of them. In the meantime, we agreed a limit for my kidney function, above which I would need dialysis. The creatinine level we agreed on was 600. If it rose to anything above that, the dialysis would start. They also put me on the list for a kidney transplant.

I remember, on the June weekend of 2003, at 5.10 in the morning, I got a telephone call telling me to come to Dublin. They said, 'We have a kidney for you.' I went off to Dublin. Strangely, for someone who hated doctors and hospitals, I was extremely calm. They did the usual blood tests and the creatinine level had risen to 600. It meant I was about to be put on the dreaded dialysis. But that day, I was given a transplant and, thank God, everything worked out fine.

It's all down to Padre Pio. When I pray to anyone, after my mother and father who are both dead, Padre Pio is the man. Any time anything goes wrong, he is the one I turn to. I don't say novenas or get involved in heavy praying. I might just say, 'Padre Pio, you're the only one that ever did anything for me. Please look down on me and help me along the way.' I might say that at home or at Mass, out for a walk or at work, but not on my hands and knees, nothing like that.

He definitely helped me the day the Franciscan arrived at the hospital in 1979. All I had prayed for that day was to go home, nothing else. I didn't pray for good results in tests. I didn't pray for any of the other men in the room. All I wanted was to get out of hospital. Having been two days short of six weeks there, I had had enough. All I could picture was the undertaker coming to collect me in the morgue to bring me home and I'd be dead at 20 years of age.

I also know he was with me when I got the transplant. All I asked him was, 'Padre Pio, protect me, keep me safe and make sure everything will be alright.' I had the operation at three o'clock. I came out of it at six and was back in the ward at seven. From that day on, everything has been fine. My creatinine is doing well. I'm married to Margaret and have three lovely children, Eoin, Niamh and Colm, and I'm feeling great.

BRIAN, WHO LIVES IN COUNTY ARMAGH but who originally comes from County Down, outlines how, thanks to Padre Pio, his wife overcame a serious illness.

My wife started getting terrible headaches in 1979, around the time when Pope John Paul II visited Ireland. They were very intense. We didn't know what was happening. The doctor initially put them down to migraine. The following year, 1980, things came to a head when she collapsed. She was speaking to another person when, the next thing, she hit the floor. She first said to the person, 'I can't hear what you are saying.' Then she fell down.

She was eventually admitted to the Royal Victoria Hospital in Belfast. They did tests there and diagnosed an aneurysm. The doctor laid out her prognosis in percentages: he said she would have a 60:40 chance of success, primarily because she was young. However, he also said, 'We don't really know until we operate and get in there.'

They operated on 1 May 1980. She was on the operating table for seven or eight hours. They found the blood vessel that had burst and they put a little clip on it. To this day, you can still see where they operated, just underneath the hairline on the left. The operation was declared a success and she made a great recovery. She had been lucky; she could have died.

It was around that time that Padre Pio first came into our lives. Although my wife had been drifting in and out of consciousness, she remembered that a relative had come to visit her the night before the operation and brought a Padre Pio mitten with him. As it happened, it was a brother of mine who had known someone who knew someone else and he had got the mitten and brought it in.

At the time, my wife wasn't into Padre Pio; nor was I. In fact, I knew nothing about him. I was a Mass-goer and would have prayed, but I was never a very religious person; religion just never grabbed me. There was, however, devotion to him in the family and I had a cousin who was a big devotee. As a result, we heard a lot more about him after the operation and we attributed great significance to the arrival of the mitten in the hospital and the success of my wife's operation.

One day, not long afterwards, my wife was in Dundalk and she went into a shop. There was a picture on sale there of Padre Pio. She said, 'I'll buy it.' Whatever the price was, that was exactly the amount of money she had in her purse. She brought it home and we put it up on a pine dresser in the kitchen. It was on the top of the dresser, leaning back towards the wall, behind a bowl. That's where it sat for the moment.

Approximately 12 months after the operation, my wife became unwell once more. She felt something strange happening in her head and she became alarmed. She wasn't well and feared that everything was starting all over again. She started going into what could only be described as trances. When she went into one, she could hear you but she couldn't respond.

She went back to the hospital and was diagnosed as having temporal lobe epilepsy. They put her on very strong tablets, which they said she would be on for the rest of her life. Unfortunately, they caused a lot of side-effects and the trances continued. She also couldn't walk 25 or 30 yards without difficulty. She became very frustrated and fed up.

One day, a strange thing happened. My wife was sitting in the front room of our house, where she was talking to her sister. I was there as well. Suddenly, we heard this awful crash in the back kitchen. It sounded like the whole dresser had come down. I went out to the kitchen to see what had happened.

What I discovered was most strange. The kitchen floor was made of ceramic tiles and the Padre Pio picture my wife had bought in Dundalk had fallen onto it. It had come the whole way down from the top shelf, out over the bowl in front of it, and it had landed face up without the glass cracking. I remember thinking, 'Something is happening here!' To me, that was the start of our intense interest in Padre Pio.

We decided, at that stage, to go to San Giovanni, to the shrine of Padre Pio. We got two cancellation tickets. Although my wife wasn't able to walk much, we travelled first to Rome and then on to San Giovanni. She was having a lot of difficulty walking and was dragging herself along. She was feeling very poorly.

Everything that happened in San Giovanni left me in no doubt that something was taking place. For a start, on one occasion, when I was in the church, I got the intense smell of perfume. The following day, when I was doing the Stations of the Cross, I got the smell again. Initially, I thought it must have come from one of the ladies, so I dropped way behind, but the perfume stayed. It gave me a great sense of elation.

What was interesting about the smell was that I had no expectation that anyone might get it. I hadn't read about it beforehand. I had expected nothing. Yet here I was getting this really wonderful perfume, like someone putting a bunch of flowers in front of your nose and then taking it away again. It was there one second and, the next second, it was gone. It was quite amazing.

After the Stations of the Cross were finished, I had a word with a Capuchin brother and I asked him what might have been happening. I remember he said to me, 'You obviously came here with a request. It's looking very good for you. The chances are that your request is going to be granted.' I asked him, 'What should I do?' He said, 'When you go home, you should do something for Padre Pio.' I promised myself, there and then, that I would.

I think it was the following day that we went on a trip to a little mountain village nearby. Like everyone else, we got off the bus and rambled through the streets. Unfortunately, my sense of direction completely deserted me and we got lost. I was confused about the way back to the bus. There we were in a mountain village, without the language and not able to ask anyone about what to do! Luckily enough, some locals recognised we were lost and directed us back.

It was only after we got to the bus that it struck us that my wife had been walking for half an hour or three-quarters of an hour and had no bother at all. She had been walking as well as me. I asked her, 'How are you feeling?' She answered, 'No bother at all.' She never had a problem walking after that. Once we returned home, we threw away her tablets and she never looked back. She is fine to this day.

After we arrived home, we started working for Padre Pio. We organised film shows about him in the local cinema and they were packed. We got a Padre Pio mitt, which people look for from far and wide. For 30 years, I organised trips to the Padre Pio weekend at Knock. I also must have taken groups of people to Rome and San Giovanni about 20 times, to give something back.

Looking back at what happened, I am certain that Padre Pio changed everything for my wife. It was mainly through his intercession that she got better. Of course, it wasn't just him; it was the man above that brought the cure, but his work was in there somewhere. I believe the key moment was that day walking in that village near San Giovanni. That was the day my wife finally got well, thanks to Padre Pio. I have no doubt about that.

Early Years

Tessie, from County Tipperary, experienced a visitation from Padre Pio shortly after her husband was diagnosed with cancer. An extraordinary development ensued.

My husband Martin became very sick in 1979. At first, they thought it was something wrong with his throat, maybe an allergy. They eventually sent him to a local hospital, where they took scans. They found that the problem was cancer in his lungs. He was coughing up blood and he wasn't well at all. Although he had been very fit and healthy, he was losing weight and had become very thin and was getting tired. They said he would need an operation in Dublin, which he didn't want to do.

Before he was due to go to Dublin, someone said, 'Why don't you take him to Tom Cooney?' Tom lived in County Clare, had met Padre Pio and had relics belonging to him. So we went to see Tom and he blessed Martin with the relics. He also said prayers. I felt there was a change in Martin right away. He hadn't wanted to go to Dublin; he was so worried and frightened by it all. He was afraid of the operation and that he wouldn't come out of it. He had said, 'I'd prefer to die at home.' But he was much better after our visit to Tom Cooney.

I didn't have any great devotion to Padre Pio at the time. We had only sought out the relic because someone else had suggested it. I hadn't known very much about him and wasn't that interested. Martin was the same. However, Tom told us about meeting Padre Pio and how he had picked him out of a group he was with on a visit to San Giovanni. He was very honoured and became a lifelong devotee. After that, I was praying that Martin would get over his cancer and that he would be alright.

We came home after the visit, which happened about a week before the operation was due to take place in Dublin. We went to bed that night. I woke up at one stage and felt that Martin was very uneasy. I checked that he was alright and brought him a drink. After that, I got up at about seven o'clock in the morning. Martin got up, too, and went to the bathroom to wash. I then went into the kitchen and was heading to the bathroom to see if he was alright.

As I was coming into the kitchen, Padre Pio was in front of me. He was standing there, as real as in life, not even a couple of feet away. He was dressed in his brown robes and had a lovely smile on his face. His eyes were narrow because he was smiling. He had grey hair and a beard and was in his 60s. I never saw what he was wearing on his feet; it was the face I was mostly looking at.

He never said anything. He just stood there, with his hands out in front of him. I never said anything either. I was so shocked, I couldn't do anything. Although I could have touched him, I didn't. I just stood there and stared at him. I was frozen and didn't say anything. It all lasted a few minutes and then Padre Pio was gone. I don't even know how he left; he just disappeared. I was suddenly there on my own.

I went on in to Martin, who was still in the bathroom, to see if he was alright. He hadn't seen or heard anything, so I brought him out into the kitchen and told him what had happened. Martin became upset and didn't know what to make of it. He was so shocked that he wasn't able to talk. I was weak. After that, the two of us were crying, even though we didn't know what we were crying over. I think we were crying with joy.

A week afterwards, Martin went up to Dublin to have his

Early Years

operation. I think what had happened encouraged him and gave him the strength to go. I went with him. They did the tests beforehand. They did scans and X-rays. They could find nothing. There was no sign of anything. Everything was gone and there was nothing to treat. He never had an operation. Martin was telling everyone, 'Padre Pio saved my life!'

Martin came back home to Tipperary after that. He was fine and lived a normal life. He wasn't sick anymore. He was well. He did, however, get some pains in his chest, but they were found to have nothing to do with cancer. Understandably, we had great devotion to Padre Pio afterwards. I know that my seeing him was real; I certainly wasn't dreaming. As a result, we covered the house with his pictures; they are everywhere.

From then on, we prayed to Padre Pio every day. We would say the Rosary to him, mostly at night. I went to Mass every morning. I also went to San Giovanni about seven or eight times; Martin went there once. We told everyone what had happened; some wouldn't believe it and had terrible doubts, while others were very interested and believed it. I felt that he was guiding our lives after that.

Eventually, about two years later, Martin got sick again, but it wasn't cancer. He got pneumonia and had pains in his back. He went downhill. He was getting a lot of colds and getting tired and weak and not looking well. He got very bad and he wasn't able to get up. He then passed away from pneumonia.

At the time of his cancer diagnosis, I think that Padre Pio intervened on Martin's behalf. Going to Tom Cooney changed everything. I was hoping that God would do something, yet I didn't think it would turn out that way. But Padre Pio can do anything you ask him to do. Sometimes, he might be a bit slow, but he will do it in time. That's what happened with Martin. I believe the cancer was there and then it was gone, thanks to Padre Pio.

MIDDLE YEARS

Salerno is located on the beautiful south-west seaboard of Italy, close to the popular Amalfi Coast. In 1995, a miracle is said to have occurred there, thanks to Padre Pio. The story, involving a mother of three children named Consiglia de Martino, resulted in the friar's beatification in 1999.

Events began to unfold on the night of 31 October when Consiglia experienced chills, pains in her chest and a feeling of suffocation. The following day, the symptoms intensified. On checking in a mirror, she saw that a swelling the size of a grapefruit had appeared in her neck.

Having been rushed to hospital, the doctors diagnosed 'a diffuse lymphatic spilling of approximately two litres caused by a rupture of the lymphatic canals.' The prognosis was bad; the outcome potentially fatal. Surgery was advised.

Consiglia, who was a devotee of Padre Pio, decided to make an immediate appeal for his help. She telephoned the friary at San Giovanni Rotondo, which she had visited on numerous occasions. There she spoke to one of the Capuchin brothers who had once known Padre Pio and asked him to pray for her at his tomb. That's what he did, he later confirmed.

By the following day, the fluid deposits in Consiglia's neck had significantly reduced and the pain had diminished. By the next day again, the swelling had all but gone. Within a week, it had completely disappeared. A comparison of CAT scans confirmed the recovery. She was sent home with a clean bill of health.

Consiglia de Martino's revival was eventually notified to the Congregation for the Causes of Saints. A medical assessment of her case concluded that her cure was 'extraordinary and scientifically inexplicable.' Her case, which was declared a miracle and attributed to Padre Pio's intercession, led to his beatification by Pope John Paul II, in May 1999, with Consiglia present at the ceremony.

Throughout the 1990s, and even back into the early 1980s, intense pressure had been exerted by Italian and Irish devotees for the beatification of Padre Pio. Proponents based their case primarily on the miracles and cures that seemingly followed prayers for his intervention or blessings with his mittens and gloves. These remarkable revivals were reported in Ireland perhaps even more than anywhere else, as the following case histories illustrate.

CONNIE, FROM COUNTY GALWAY, overcame a heart condition, thanks to Padre Pio.

I was born in 1980 without a chamber in my heart, so I had only three chambers in all. Initially, my mother thought I was normal, but at six weeks I wasn't thriving, so she brought me to the doctor. I was sent straight to hospital and she was told there was nothing they could do. Basically, there was a huge hole in my heart. The prognosis was poor. Not many babies in my state would survive in those days, so I was sent home to die.

They did surgery on me when I was about six months old. My mother was then told to tube feed me at home and there was no appointment made to go back. I did, however, put on a pound in weight, so they thought, 'God! This one is putting

Middle Years

on weight, so we should give her a chance.' They put me on medication and kept me coming back.

My parents were devastated by what was happening. There were two very small babies at home – my two brothers – so they had a lot on their hands. At the time, over three decades ago, there were few phones around and I was in hospital in Dublin on my own. My father was looking after the boys at home, while my mother was trying to travel up and down to Dublin.

At one stage, when I was about one-and-a-half or two years old, I got a massive heart attack. I was in hospital when it happened and they called Mam. She rushed to the hospital, but by the time she got there I was fine, although my prospects were still bad. I can't imagine what I would do now if the roles were reversed and my child was in the same position.

My mother decided that she wasn't going to listen to the doctors, so she brought me home and fed me and kept feeding me. I went to school as normal and travelled to Dublin every year for a check-up. I did everything I was supposed to do as a normal child. I would walk to school in the morning. I did my basketball. I was pure stubborn and I wouldn't give in to anyone.

I did feel a bit tired and my hands and lips were blue. That went on right through school. If anybody said anything, I'd just ignore them. I remember, one day, a fellow called me 'blue lips,' but he didn't get too many nice things said back to him. Although very few people said anything, I was very conscious of myself. But I got on with life and did well.

Padre Pio was always there throughout that time and Mam always had great faith in him. Because of him, she always knew I was going to be OK. Whenever she asked for anything, she received it. She would say, 'I'm not going to listen to the doctors, no matter what they say. They really think they know everything, but they don't. Padre Pio knows more.'

He was always in her life. She prayed to him constantly and she went to prayer meetings. She said novenas. I always remember seeing photographs of him in the house when I was growing up. We got the magazines and they would always be around the place. He was a name that we spoke of at home. We also watched his canonisation on television. Padre Pio was always there, a big part of our lives. She said he was the only reason I was around.

Eventually, in 2006, I got married and wanted to start a family. Unfortunately, I was told that I would never have a child because of my condition. My cardiologist said no, but I wasn't going to take no for an answer. I wanted a baby as I loved being married and had a lovely husband. I said to myself, 'I'm not going to let this stop me.'

I decided there was nothing for it but to go to San Giovanni and ask Padre Pio for help. I went with Mam. We went in January and made our own way. We flew to Rome and took the train to Foggia and then got the bus to San Giovanni. It was a long trip, but I felt I had to go. I went to Mass there and prayed at the tomb. We did the Stations of the Cross. It was lovely, absolutely fabulous.

Not long after I came back, I got pregnant and had a little boy of my own in 2009. Although the baby was born early and I was in hospital for a long time, my son ended up being fine. He's now a wonderful, thriving child. I got everything else I asked for in San Giovanni, too. I asked that I could sell a business and I got a buyer. We had a car we couldn't sell and we sold it. The big three things I asked for all happened. I put it all down to Padre Pio.

I went back to San Giovanni in 2012 to thank him and to ask for his help again. I was told I had to have heart surgery and I didn't want to have it. I was experiencing rapid heart rates and the cardiologist said, 'Once these things start, they are a sign that things aren't going as well as we had hoped. Surgery is the only option.' They said the surgery would give me more energy and improve my colour.

More than anything, I didn't want surgery. They told me they were organising an MRI, but I said I wouldn't have it until after I went to San Giovanni. I went there and the following week I had my MRI. It turned out that I did have to have the surgery. I went to a lady in Galway, who has a Padre Pio glove, and she said, 'Maybe it's meant to be.' I started thinking, 'Well, maybe it is. Maybe this is Padre Pio's plan for me.'

On the morning prior to the surgery, I went to Mass in the hospital. I was just sitting down on a seat. Something told me to turn to my left. I did so. And whose picture was staring at me, almost straight into my eyes? It was a picture of Padre Pio! I rang Mam straight away and said, 'You'll never guess what's just happened!'

I had the surgery and it worked out perfectly. I'm not blue anymore. I have energy. I can do exercises I could never do before. I can run up the stairs now and not even think about it, whereas before I couldn't. What I always wanted was to be normal, like everyone else, and I am.

All that matters is that I can live a normal life and that's what I always asked for. I waited three decades for this to happen and it's happened. It's all down to Padre Pio. He is amazing. I know, in my heart and soul, what he has done for me. And I know he is always there to help me, no matter what.

Elizabeth, from County Kerry, tells of a remarkable young boy who, while dying from leukaemia, claimed to have been visited by Padre Pio. The event happened in the early 1980s.

Three of us formed a Padre Pio prayer group in our town many decades ago. I am the last alive of the three, but the group is still going strong. In 1981, we decided to go on a trip to Rome and then on to San Giovanni. It was the first of a number of trips we made to San Giovanni and we raised enough money to take three children with us.

One of the children was a little boy who had leukaemia and was about six or seven years of age. He was a very quiet, shy boy. His hair was gone and he was on medication. Sometimes, he found the trip hard because of his illness. He was sick the whole time, probably from his medication. I remember there wasn't a lot he could eat. But he was amazing, a lovely young lad and a very good child. Although he was sick, he never cried or did anything like that.

At the time, it wasn't long after Padre Pio had died. In San Giovanni, they took us to see the clothes he wore while saying Mass. They showed us the little room he had slept in and the confessional where he heard confessions. We saw his habits and gloves and we could touch them. They told us how the Devil would come into Padre Pio's room at night and beat him up. They even laid the little boy with leukaemia on Padre Pio's bed.

As it happened, the little fellow had never been an altar boy.

Middle Years

In almost every little church we were in, while we were away, the priest would say Mass and that little boy would act as altar boy. I don't think he ever made a mistake. He was able to ring the bell at the Consecration. I think he served Mass about three or four times, in different churches, although not in San Giovanni, and he was delighted with himself helping the priest.

When he came back home to Kerry, he was alright for a while, but then he became really sick and was confined to bed. At some stage, he lost his speech and wasn't able to talk. I don't know why that happened. But he had other ways of communicating and he could let his mother know what was going on; he just couldn't communicate through speech.

On one occasion, a friend of mine and I were invited by the boy's mother to go up to the house to visit him. He was sleeping downstairs, with one of the main rooms turned into a bedroom. People could more easily come in to visit with it set up that way. When we went into his room, he was in a bad mood, so we went to the kitchen for a cup of tea. After a while, his mother said, 'Come on in, he's smiling again.' So we went back in.

As soon as we had entered, the mother asked him, 'Tell me once again who visited you last night. Who was the lovely man who came to visit?' Although he couldn't speak, he had this photograph of Padre Pio under his pillow. The photo was on one of those religious leaflets. He put his hand under the pillow and he pulled it out and pointed at it. His mother said, 'Is that who called to see you?' He kept pointing at it, making it clear that it was.

His mother also told us that, at another time, she and her aunt were in the room with him and were quite close to the bed. He kept pushing them away. He would motion as if to say, 'Move back! Move back!' They didn't know what was going on or what was wrong with him. His eyes were moving around the room, mostly around the bed, and he was beaming. It looked as if he thought they were getting in the way of someone else who seemed to be walking around the bed. They felt Padre Pio was with him.

His mother also told us that, on another occasion, she was upstairs making the bed and she heard her front gate either shutting or opening. She looked out the window and saw a Franciscan or a Capuchin coming in. The person was dressed in a habit. Her aunt was downstairs with the little boy at the time. She waited a few minutes and went down to join them. She said to her aunt, 'Where's the Franciscan?' Her aunt said, 'There's no Franciscan here.' Yet she had seen him opening the gate and coming in. It was very strange.

Looking back, I believe Padre Pio came to that little boy. I think that he must have seen him. I don't think that children of that age would sound so convincing if they weren't telling the truth. They might pretend that they saw something, but you would know they were telling a fib. Yet he was convincing and it was clear he saw someone. You would believe what he was trying to tell you. I certainly believed him anyway. He was so honest about it.

That beautiful boy died about six months after that and, somehow, I think Padre Pio was with him all the time. He came home with him from San Giovanni, you could say. I'd also say that he went to Padre Pio after he died. He certainly believed in him and, in the graveyard, they have Padre Pio on his headstone.

What had happened confirmed my beliefs. I went to San

Giovanni a few times afterwards and I remained with the prayer group. I still have Padre Pio's photograph in my kitchen, in my bathroom, in my bedroom; he's all over the place. I really believe in him and I ask him to help me. Just like he helped that little boy, I know he always helps me, too.

EILEEN, FROM COUNTY KERRY, attributes her son's recovery from a serious brain virus to the intervention of Padre Pio. The event dates back to 1981.

My son, who was six going on seven years old, got very sick at home. He had a cough and I took him to the doctor on a Friday evening. I thought it might have been whooping cough, but the doctor said, 'You never know until they whoop.' He was put on antibiotics as he seemed to have a bit of a chest infection.

I kept him home from school on the Monday. He seemed to be in good form during the day, so much so that he was due to stay with a friend on the Monday evening. He said he fell at the friend's house, so he came back home and he was very sick that night. He whooped and he vomited and he was very irritable.

Coming into the next morning, he started to become confused. He just didn't know where he was and he didn't even really recognise me. I took him to the hospital. He was very ill and was getting worse and worse. At this stage, he was almost in a coma. They eventually told us that he had developed a brain inflammation caused by a virus, which is known as encephalitis. It was very serious.

He needed to be put into a private room because of the whooping cough. He was isolated in the room and received intensive care there. Nurses and a doctor were with him all the time. A neurologist was involved and they started giving him medication. He was attached to drips. We were put into a room beside him and were left with the impression that he could die or if he lived he would be brain-damaged. I think they felt he wasn't going to make it.

He then started getting fits or convulsions. They were like epileptic fits. He got the first as he was being taken for a CAT scan. It was terrifying to see. We were walking with him along the corridor. I could see a change coming over him. He was getting a seizure and they ran with him into a room where he had to be given oxygen. It was lucky that he was so close to the oxygen when it happened.

Eventually, he was brought back to his room and kept in isolation. Even we didn't get to see him. The hospital staff suggested that we shouldn't go in to him because of the fits; they said they were quite terrifying and it would be a memory that we would be better off not witnessing as it would stay with us for the rest of our lives. So we stayed in our room and waited.

By then, word had got out back home that our son was very ill. The local curate, who had great faith in Padre Pio, knew of a man in Cork who had a mitten of Padre Pio and he contacted him. We knew nothing about it, but apparently the man came in around midnight a few days after my son was admitted to the hospital. We only heard about the visit in the morning. At around seven o'clock, we were told by the doctor who was with him the previous night.

The doctor said that the man had come in with a Padre Pio glove and blessed our son and prayed with him. She also told us that, as soon as the man came in, things started to improve. The gaps between the fits became longer and longer. Instead of

Middle Years

getting them every minute or two minutes, he was getting them every five minutes. I think she was amazed and surprised by what had happened.

Although he was still in a coma, our son started to recover immediately. Very quickly, the fits stopped altogether. They still said that it would be 48 hours before they'd know if he would come out of it or if he had brain damage. But the improvement was important because, at that stage, he was very weak and you would wonder how much more he could take. He was, after all, only a frail little boy and six years old.

Later that day, he started to come out of the coma. He improved slowly. At first, he started to blink or yawn or to move his finger or hand. There might be a couple of hours between each sign of an improvement, but all the movements were significant because they meant that there was some brain activity there. He recovered quickly after that and within two weeks he was back home and perfect again. He literally went from dying to being given hope and to getting well.

We were delighted and we regarded what had happened as a miracle. I don't know if, at the time, we associated what happened completely with Padre Pio. You have to remember that our son's room was like a shrine with all the relics people gave us. There were many saints represented. We weren't even into Padre Pio at the time. But the fact that the doctor told us that as soon as the man came in our son started to improve persuaded us that Padre Pio was involved.

Later, either a doctor or a priest told us that our son was the biggest miracle to ever come out of the hospital. Since then, I have prayed to Padre Pio, although I wouldn't say I am over-religious. However, I do have devotion to him. I always say a simple little prayer: 'Padre Pio, pray for us. Thank you for looking after us, and please continue to do so.' My son, who was sick, has devotion to him, too.

Ever since what happened, we've had a picture of Padre Pio in the house and we have little relic cards of him as well. We even used Pia as one of my daughter's names after she was born. Later, we met the man who brought the relic to the hospital and we told him our story. But he wasn't in the least bit surprised. He had come across lots of similar stories and had heard of many miracles and cures just like our own.

CATHERINE, FROM COUNTY WESTMEATH, recollects how her son's eye problem was cured after he was blessed with a Padre Pio glove.

I had a Down syndrome boy born to me in July 1984. I knew when I was pregnant that something was wrong. I knew it in my heart, like there was some sort of weight there. It must have been a mother's instinct. I said it to the doctors, but they just fobbed me off.

They told me straight after he was born what was wrong. They asked me, 'Do you know what Down syndrome is?' I said, 'Yes.' They then said, 'Well, your son has Down syndrome.' I was very upset and wondered how I would rear the child. You feel you know how to do things when you have a normal child, but you worry about rearing a child with special needs.

They were wonderful in the hospital. A doctor came in and sat with me for about six hours and told me what to expect. One of the first things that came into my mind was, 'My son will never get married.' An awful lot of people with special needs children think that. I also wondered, 'How will we cope? What will I have to do differently to rear him?'

From the beginning, my son had a problem with his eye.

His left eye was turned to the side, while his other eye would focus straight ahead. The crooked eye was very bad. I was told that he would need to be operated on when he was two years old; they wouldn't operate until then. I was very worried about what he would have to go through. I didn't want him to suffer.

That's when Padre Pio came into my life. I was still in the hospital when my mother-in-law came to visit. She wasn't really into Padre Pio and knew nothing about him. However, her daughter had been at an event in a hall and had won a little picture of him. The first thing my mother-in-law did was to bring it to me. I thought, 'This is an omen. I must get to know Padre Pio.' I felt drawn to him. I thought, 'This is meant to be.'

I knew nothing about him at the time; he hadn't featured in our family. However, I got one of his leaflets and I started to pray to him straight away. I prayed to him for the grace to rear Aidan. I also kept the picture and I still have it to this day. It's a small, coloured photograph of his face in an oval frame. He looks lovely in it; he's smiling and a little bit older. I brought the picture home and I hung it in my son's room.

I then heard about Padre Pio's glove. I had known nothing about that either. At this stage, Aidan was about a year-and-a-half or two years old. I made enquiries and heard that a woman had one. I heard that the glove had been worn by Padre Pio and I knew it was important. I was told it caused miracles to happen. I felt, 'I need to go to it.'

I got the woman's phone number and I went to see her. I can remember travelling up by car, with a friend driving. I brought my son with me. We found the house and knocked on the door. The woman was lovely and she invited us in. I explained to her how my son's eye was crooked and that I was concerned about it. She said, 'Let's bless his eyes with the glove.'

She handed the glove to me to bless Aidan. I sat down and put him on my knee. I blessed his eyes with it. I don't think I prayed at the time, although the woman might have. Instead, I asked Padre Pio that my son's eye would be healed. I had deep faith that something would happen and great belief that the glove would work.

After I blessed Aidan, I was having a little chat with the woman. I suddenly looked into his eyes and his two eyes were looking forward. The crookedness was gone! The eyes were perfect. Straight away, he was inexplicably healed and I had no doubt I had just witnessed a miracle.

It was all so wonderful. The woman was delighted and so was I. We thanked God and Padre Pio and Our Lady. Although we were a bit shocked, I had kind of expected it to happen. I had the belief that he would be cured and that's what had happened. It really was so wonderful and I knew the crooked eye was gone forever and would never return.

Afterwards, I told everyone about what had taken place. They were amazed. They felt that it was a miracle, too. I also brought him to an optician to get an eye test done when he was about three or three-and-a-half. I told the optician that his eye had been crooked. 'There was never anything wrong with his eye,' he said. He was amazed that there had ever been a problem. That was proof again, not that I needed it.

I got further proof of Padre Pio's powers, later on, regarding my mother and father. Daddy had prostate cancer and they gave him maybe a year to a year-and-a-half to live. My mother's neighbour gave her a relic of Padre Pio and Mammy blessed

Middle Years

Daddy with it. He was healed and he lived for another 25 years.

Mammy later had a heart attack. After it, she developed a phobia where she could never go anywhere without me. Even when she went shopping, I had to be with her. I gave her a Padre Pio leaflet and said, 'Mammy, say that prayer and he will help you.' She started praying with the leaflet. Almost immediately, she got this beautiful smell of perfume. She ran back to me and told me. I said, 'That's Padre Pio's perfume. You are healed.' The next time she went shopping, she went on her own.

Nothing surprises me with Padre Pio. I have no doubt he causes miracles to happen. I definitely know Aidan was cured by him and that he was saved the pain of having to have an operation. It is also strange how, to this day, Aidan's eyes are very like Padre Pio's. They have the same shape and look. He also has the big eyebrows, like Padre Pio had. I'm not the only one who says that; my friends see it, too.

As life goes on, I appreciate what God has sent me with my son. He's a special person, who has brought me a lot of laughter. He's brilliant. You love all your children, but I love him differently. Most people who have special needs children will tell you that. You are probably more protective and they need that bit more attention. I believe that's a gift from God.

I now think Padre Pio is wonderful. To this day, 27 years since my son was cured, I am a devotee of his. I give out leaflets about him and I still pray to him. He's a wonderful saint. He answered my prayers and also brought my son a gift. What happened was simple: my son's eyes were crooked and, after being blessed with the glove, he came home with his eyes straight.

MAIRÉAD, FROM COUNTY CAVAN, tells of Padre Pio's role in the disappearance of her daughter's hole in the heart.

It all happened when my daughter Deirdre was born back in October 1984. She was born with a hole in her heart. They told us that the hole was very large and they didn't hold out that much hope for her. They advised us to bring her home and said, 'If she gets very bad and turns blue, bring her straight back in.' The hospital were more or less telling us, 'Bring her home and see what happens.' And that's what we did.

After that, we were up and down to the Children's Hospital in Crumlin, having X-rays and tests done on Deirdre's heart. They showed us what it was like. It was enlarged on one side. What was happening was that there was a hole between the right and left ventricles in the bottom part of her heart. As a result, the blood, rather than flowing up in the usual direction, was hitting off the side of her heart and making it bulge. It didn't look normal.

We were devastated and very upset. We thought we were going to lose her and we prayed that we wouldn't. Every night, we worried that she was going to turn blue. We were also worried that she might have to have an operation; she was so tiny and we thought she wouldn't come through it. Her consultant didn't know whether to operate or not, as he wasn't sure if an operation was appropriate. He couldn't make up his mind.

One night, in the wintertime, we had a knock on the door and it was a man who offered to bring us a Padre Pio cap. I had known of Padre Pio since long before then, back to when I was a child of about eight or nine. He was alive at that stage. My aunt had great faith in him. I remember she told me about

Middle Years

him and she said, 'If you went into confession with him, he'd know your sins. You wouldn't have to tell him because he could see into your heart and soul.' I was amazed and what she said stuck with me. My husband's mother also had great faith in Padre Pio.

Probably because of that, when we were asked if we wanted Padre Pio's cap to be brought to Deirdre, we immediately said yes. The man and his wife eventually brought it around. I remember it was a dark, horrible night. It was just a little black skull cap, which Padre Pio had worn. The man duly put it on Deirdre.

Our other children thought it looked funny and were kind of laughing. I thought, 'This isn't going to work because the children aren't being very reverent.' Anyway, we all knelt down in our sitting-room, as a family, and we prayed to Padre Pio. After that, we put all our trust in him and we prayed that he would make her live. That started the devotion which my husband and I have to this day.

One night, a couple of years later, a strange thing happened. Deirdre, who was then around three years old, was sleeping in the same room as Áine, another daughter who was ten years older than her. In the morning, Áine told me that Deirdre got up during the night. She crawled down to the bottom of the bed and said, 'There's a man in the room!' She said, 'Do you see the man?' But Áine saw nothing.

Áine then put on the light and still couldn't see anything. In the morning, she said, 'Deirdre was definitely looking at something.' Apparently, she had crawled down to the bottom of the bed and was looking and staring as if somebody, or something, was there. Áine said it was all very strange.

As it happens, I have a picture of Padre Pio on my dressing-table and, some time later, Deirdre was with me while I was making the bed. She saw the picture and said, 'I saw that man in my room! That man was with me in my room!' I got such a shock. It made me think it had to be Padre Pio who was in the room with her. I think she was really too young to have made up what she said, but she was old enough to say it.

Not long after that, we were scheduled to visit the consultant up in Dublin and we prayed and prayed the night before that Deirdre wouldn't need an operation. I can remember we went up early in the morning and she had all the X-rays and the cardiograms and things like that.

We eventually arrived in her consultant's room. He got all the results and reports together and then said, 'She will never have to have an operation. The hole has closed up.' What had happened was that her heart was growing but the hole wasn't growing along with it, so it was getting smaller and smaller in comparison to the size of her heart. We were so relieved.

Ever since then, Deirdre has been fine. She was just like a normal girl growing up. She was very lively and cheerful and happy. The doctor in Crumlin told us, 'She can do whatever she wants. She can even go for the Olympics if she wants to,' so she was active and joined in the school sports. She took part in everything that was happening. Today, she is in her late 20s, married and is a wonderful daughter. Everything has been great ever since.

There was another recovery associated with our family. My husband, Laurence, has a nephew who had to have a bag attached to him as a baby. This was about six or seven years after Deirdre. We got the cap again, as the baby was very, very ill. Once more, on a dark, cold night, we brought the cap to their house. When we got there, they were crying because they couldn't get the bag to attach to his side. The baby was screaming as well.

After we arrived, we all knelt down and put the cap on the little fellow. He was screaming when we did it. But, all of a sudden, he stopped and they got the bag on. Everything settled down after that and we returned the cap. From then on, the news was all good. That fellow is now a smashing young man, just into his 20s. I believe Padre Pio had a role in that, too.

Looking back, I believe Padre Pio intervened for Deirdre and made her well. I begged him to make her better and I believed that he would. I really think the arrival of the cap was the turning point. That marked the change. She did so well from then on. I put it down to him.

As a result, we went over to Rome for his canonisation. We also went twice to San Giovanni to say thanks. We still pray to him and believe in him all the time. I light a candle to him every morning after I get up. I have never forgotten what he did for Deirdre and I will always be grateful to him for the blessing he brought us. He certainly delivers.

ELIZABETH, FROM COUNTY WATERFORD, describes her cancer surgery and a strange transformation that happened following the arrival of a Padre Pio glove.

In 1985, I was diagnosed with a tumour on a kidney. I had found out beforehand that I had a double kidney on one side and a single on the other, so I had previous issues with them, but nothing major. This time, however, I was in constant pain and was generally debilitated. I didn't fear it was cancer. Nobody talked about cancer back then; the only people I ever knew who had it had died and I never associated it with me.

I was sent off immediately to Dublin and had scans and tests. I remember, afterwards, the doctor came in and said, 'You have a lump!' I thought, 'What a strange word to use.' It was a shocking term. I said, 'Do you mean cancer?' He said, 'Yes.' It turned out I had a tumour on the kidneys, on the left. I nearly died with the shock. The only other thing he said was, 'You'll have to have surgery.' He never informed me what my chances were.

I was told this coming up to the weekend and the surgery was arranged for the Monday. The weekend was horrific. I remember friends coming and taking me out for a drive. I was so traumatised that it didn't matter where I went or what I did. It wasn't that the surgery bothered me; it was just that I was afraid I was going to die. I was in my mid-30s at the time and having a good old life and suddenly this had happened.

I had surgery on the Monday and they took two kidneys out. I think it was that evening when the doctor came back in. He was quite stressed and wasn't feeling good about things. He said, 'Yes, it was cancer, but we don't know where it has spread. You will have to have further surgery.' I thought, 'This is definitely it!' The surgery was going to be in the following few days, after I had recovered from the first one.

Just as the doctor was leaving, my father and brother came in carrying a Padre Pio glove. A relation of mine in Waterford knew a priest in Dublin who had access to a glove. My father had been told to go and collect it, which he did. The glove meant very little to me. I knew of Padre Pio in a vague way, but nothing more. Although I had basic beliefs and tried to live a good life, I had no great faith.

I just sat there with the glove. I think I held it in my hand or put it on my tummy or whatever. I don't think I even said a prayer. I certainly didn't believe, 'This is going to cure me.' There was nothing like that and there was no delight that I was holding one of Padre Pio's gloves. There were other ladies in my room, who were very ill, and I offered it to them, but neither was remotely interested either.

The glove had to be returned within the hour and I probably had it for half an hour. Just as my father was leaving with it, the doctor came back in. The two of them literally passed one another on the corridor. This time, the doctor was a completely different man, with a completely different attitude. He said, 'I have great news, the cancer hasn't spread, although you will have to have another little operation.' I recall that the other operation involved one of the ureters or something, but it was small.

I have no idea what had taken place: whether the doctor had just got news from the lab saying the cancer hadn't spread or whether, on the first visit, he was only guessing I would need further surgery. Either way, he was a very different man. There had been a huge change of attitude within half an hour. The further surgery was nothing and it wasn't an issue. What had happened was extraordinary and it gave me a great lift. A huge weight was taken off my shoulders.

I immediately made a connection between the news and the arrival of the glove. Within the half an hour that I'd had the glove, my doctor's attitude was transformed. I felt the timing was very significant. The first time he was bringing me bad news and the second time he was bringing me good news. What had taken place seemed remarkable to me at the time. Ten days later, I had the further surgery and I went home.

In time, my doctor moved to the States for further study and I was assigned to a different doctor in the same hospital. I would have to go to him every three months for a check-up. I think on the first time I went to him he said, 'Oh, here's the miracle woman!' I never asked him what he meant, but clearly word had spread that I had an unusual or miraculous recovery. I never had any problems after that, no chemotherapy and no radiotherapy, apart from a tiny procedure on my leg, which was nothing.

Afterwards, at home, I didn't talk about the cancer because you never spoke about it at the time. But I did tell people close to me about what had happened. They would say, 'Oh, my God! Imagine!' I suppose I didn't have any proof of a miracle or anything like that, but the timing was so obvious: my father and brother brought the glove in to me after the doctor had just left; as they were leaving the doctor was on his way back in and was a different man.

From then on, I said my prayers to Padre Pio every night. I developed devotion to him. I went to prayer-group meetings for about a year, but then I went back to work. Every night, however, I prayed to Padre Pio and it would be one of the very few prayers I would be saying. I still do it; it's an ongoing thing.

My mother developed devotion to him as well. At one stage, she got a strange smell of roses. She was also convinced that she saw Padre Pio one night. She said, 'I wouldn't be saying this to anybody, but I will say it to you.' She went on to tell me how she was awake and she saw the end of his robes going out the door. She was quite bothered by it and asked me, 'Could I really have seen it?' She wouldn't be hysterical and wouldn't be given to that sort of thing at all.

My father also developed devotion to him and the three of us – my father, mother and I – went off to San Giovanni about two years after I had been sick. He had developed a 'thing' for Padre Pio following what happened to me. My father was a very quiet man, yet in Padre Pio's cell he took off his shoes, jumped over the ropes and he put Padre Pio's shoes on him. It all happened in a flash. He just saw them there and he felt compelled to do it. It was so unlike him; he was so quiet and retiring and would never do anything wrong.

We went to San Giovanni about two or three times after that. The visits didn't do much for me, as I don't greatly like pilgrimages. Whatever I have is between me and Padre Pio and the Lord or whoever. And I like to do it at home, not on a pilgrimage.

I still believe something significant happened with me. I can't choose between the medical and the miraculous, but I'm sure the timing was strange. Within half an hour, my doctor's attitude had been transformed from negative to positive. It was more than a coincidence, I think.

MARJORIE, FROM DUBLIN but who lives in Cork, recollects her daughter's devotion to Padre Pio throughout her battle with multiple sclerosis (MS).

My daughter Joan developed MS when she was 24. She was a brilliant girl, who did her college degrees and got into computers at an early stage. In 1985, we thought she had the flu and she couldn't shake it off. She was terribly tired. One morning, in work, she developed double vision. She had a scan in Dublin and, in May of that year, was diagnosed with MS.

Our local doctor was as shocked as we were. I asked him, 'What do we do now?' He said, 'We just watch and hope and pray.' There wasn't much that could be done. Her eyesight deteriorated very quickly. She then started to drag a leg. The MS was progressive and it went into a downward spiral very rapidly.

We couldn't believe it. Joan's father had been very ill for a long time with a heart problem. One of our children was born prematurely and had problems with both hips. Another child was born with a congenital hip. They were unusual things for us to be dealing with and there was always someone needing attention. Joan was another one along the way.

At an early stage, we went to visit a lovely woman in Cork called Margot Scannell, who had a Padre Pio mitt. Lots of people went to her house to be blessed in the hope of getting better. We went to her, one evening, when Joan's eyesight was very bad. Margot said some beautiful prayers and gave Joan a blessing.

I remember, as we were coming out and standing at the doorway, Joan said to her, 'Margot, you must have gorgeous flowers in your garden. There's a most beautiful smell.' As it happened, Margot hadn't a flower in the garden. She said to Joan, 'That's Padre Pio.' After that, Joan had great devotion.

In her own way, Joan was very spiritual. I remember one of the girls who worked with her said, 'Joan, you must get very annoyed with God and ask why you should be sick like this.' But she said, 'Why would I ask God that? Why should somebody else get it instead of me?' She was also very charitable. At that stage, Romanian orphanages were in the news and she always sent money off to them. She was great like that; she never thought about herself at all.

Her sight went very quickly. Her legs gave out, along with her coordination. She was in a wheelchair and was sleeping downstairs. Her body functions didn't work. She was in pain.

Middle Years

She did, however, have a boyfriend and they became engaged. They were mad about each other and had a bungalow built to cater for her needs. But she was going downhill rapidly and they never moved in.

Joan stayed with me for four-and-a-half years. Eventually, I had to get a public health nurse in to help me as I couldn't manage any more. One morning, she came in and said, 'You'll have to make the decision to let Joan go into a hospital.' She advised me which hospital to put her into, which was run by an order of nuns. Joan was there for nine-and-a-half years. It was a long time and, God love her, she was always cheerful and never gave up hope that something would happen.

Throughout that time, she always had a photo of Padre Pio on her bedside locker or her chest of drawers. I have no doubt that she prayed to him, too. She must have wanted a cure. I think he brought peace of mind and contentment to her, even though she was never really happy with her lot. I suppose acceptance is what he ultimately gave her.

Joan lived with her MS for 14 years. For the last six of those years, she had an abdominal feeding tube inserted and from Christmas Day 1993 neither a morsel of food nor a drop of water passed her lips. She did, however, receive the host regularly and, while a drop of water could have caused major problems if it went down the wrong way, astonishingly the host was never a problem.

She was at death's door so often that it became a pattern to see her being extremely ill. One weekend, she had a slight temperature and a little chest infection which was being treated with antibiotics. This was not unusual and we were not unduly concerned. However, the hospital phoned me before seven o'clock in the morning on Tuesday, 26 January

1999 and they thought I should come up as they saw a change in her condition. I went immediately.

As I sat at the bedside, one of the nurses handed me a book on Padre Pio. She told me that one of the sisters had been using it the previous night and she thought I might like to see it. The book was compiled in the form of a calendar, with a message for every date. When I opened it, the end of the left-hand page had a message for 23 January. The facing page just had a picture of Padre Pio smiling out at me.

I turned the page, to move on to 24 and 25 January and the day I was looking for, that day, 26 January. All these days were totally missing. The next part of the book started on 29 January. In my heart, I felt there was a message there for me. As it turned out, the missing days accounted for the end of Joan's illness – 24 and 25 January – while she died on 26 January and her burial took place on 28 January.

Later that day, I was showing another daughter the gap in the book and, when I opened it at the original place – 23 January – I was surprised to find a different picture opposite it. This time, Padre Pio was turned slightly side-faced, looking sad, and had his hood up. At the hospital, they all realised the significance. I know Padre Pio was giving me a clear message.

Joan died most peacefully after nine o'clock on the night of 26 January and we were with her. I can only put what happened down to something miraculous; there's no other explanation. It was most extraordinary. I believe my daughter went to heaven and Padre Pio was with her to the end.

Middle Years

MYLES, FROM COUNTY WEXFORD, has a daughter whose mysterious childhood ailment was cured by Padre Pio. His family were living in London at the time. He also refers to Padre Pio's role in his wife's death.

My daughter was born in 1987 in Guy's Hospital in London. A couple of days after the birth, my wife got some very bad headaches, so they took the child from her for a day. A few hours after we got the baby back, we noticed little blisters coming up, spreading from her waist down to the back of her legs. The blisters were like little red marks. They would just appear, come to a head, burst and disappear, having left little marks on the skin. She would cry when they were there; they must have been scalding her. She must have been in a lot of pain.

For two months or more, we were bringing her to doctors and they couldn't find out what was wrong. We brought her home on holidays to Ireland and took her to another doctor, but he couldn't explain them either. At this stage, the child was on medicines, being rubbed with ointments and getting injections. I remember saying to my wife, 'For a child so young, she is on a huge amount of medication.' It was awful what she was going through.

We eventually returned to London and my mother-in-law came over to visit, which she often did. It was almost three months, at that stage, since the child's blisters had started. My mother-in-law was a big devotee of Padre Pio and had prayed to him all her life. She was a true believer, who went to Mass every morning, no matter how sick she was. She was also a true believer in the Rosary; she said it every night. In fact, all of her family were believers and knew of Padre Pio and what he could do.

We were telling my mother-in-law about the child and what was wrong. We had a big, brown, leather sofa in the front sitting-room and I remember one morning she said to my wife, 'Put the child lying on her face on the sofa.' My wife did so. I can still see the child lying on the sofa all these years later. I can recall the exact positions that my mother-in-law and wife were in.

The mother-in-law blessed her with holy water and Padre Pio's relic, which she had in her hands. I can't remember what sort of relic it was, but it might have been a piece of cloth. She just shook the holy water over the baby and blessed her with the relic. It all took only two or three minutes. And that was it. The blisters were gone within half an hour and they never returned since!

I was surprised and glad that they were gone. I remember saying, 'Imagine all the places we brought the child, yet it was the holy water and relic that did it!' I wasn't a great believer at the time. I worked seven days a week and on some Sundays I'd go to Mass while on others I wouldn't. If I had the belief then that I have now, I wouldn't have been so surprised because I now know the powers of Padre Pio. Thank God, I've turned that around.

Eventually, in February 2004, my wife died. She passed away from cancer of the breast and a tumour in the brain. She found a lump in her breast on 1 January 2000 and she had the breast removed in March. It was a big operation. She then got a lump in her neck and they did a biopsy. It was cancer again, which then spread to her brain. We were told there was nothing they could do, except keep it at bay for some time. Beyond that, they were helpless.

Padre Pio came into the picture again. I prayed to Our Lord that my wife wouldn't mind dying and I prayed to Padre

Middle Years

Pio that she wouldn't have any pain. It turned out that she didn't mind dying and, although she had a massive brain tumour, she had no pain. She told me on many occasions that she hadn't a pain in the world. They were two gifts that she received at the time. Every day, I prayed for them and I presume she prayed, too.

For a week before she died, every morning when I'd wake up I'd get the smell of roses. I knew it was connected to Padre Pio. But the morning she died, when I woke up I didn't get the smell until I came out in the hallway. The aroma there was incredible; it was like as if someone had sprayed an aerosol can around.

It was absolutely beautiful, yet no one else could get it even though there were a lot of people in the house. It was as if Padre Pio was waiting for her. I believe he was coming to her every morning, but that day he was waiting to bring her away. That happened early in the morning, about 7.30 or 8.00, and she died at 9.20.

After she died, I was looking in drawers and found several relics of Padre Pio that I did not know she had. They might have belonged originally to her mother, I don't know. But she was certainly praying to him and the relics are precious. I now have one of them attached to the keys of my car and, please God, I will never lose it.

After the death of my wife, I went to Medjugorje but not to San Giovanni. I have been in Medjugorje 15 times since 2004. I have great devotion to the place and I know for a fact that Our Lady appears there every day. The healings and the blessings I get there are amazing. But, even though I haven't been to San Giovanni, I still believe in Padre Pio.

I will never forget what happened, especially with my

daughter. I told my daughter the story ages ago and she was amazed. She is in her 20s now and is a fine, healthy young mother. She has never had this problem since. It never came back. Yet no doctor knew what was wrong with the child and it was only through my mother-in-law and Padre Pio that she was cured.

I believe Padre Pio has brilliant powers, through the Holy Spirit, and he does great things. I think he has great healing ability and I always pray to him, although I also pray to a lot of the saints. You really do need to believe in him, and I do. I can't imagine how you could miss him or forget him; he is such a wonderful saint. It was definitely through him that my child was healed.

TEDDY, WHO COMES FROM WEST CORK but who has lived in Cork city for over 60 years, recounts a strange story that occurred around the time of a near-tragic fire in his home.

I first saw a picture of Padre Pio when I was about eight years old. That was 70 years ago, in the early 1940s. The picture of him was on a book in a shop window in Macroom. The shop sold everything, including toys and books. I was coming home from school and I looked in the window and he was there. It was a big book with Padre Pio on the front. I saw the stigmata on his hands and I was really fascinated.

I didn't know anything about the stigmata at the time. I thought it was very strange how this could happen. I spent the week looking at the book, until it was removed. That was the last that I heard about Padre Pio for some time. I never had anything more to do with him until 1990, which was almost 50 years later.

What happened in 1990 was that my house caught fire.

Middle Years

It was the time of the World Cup and we had just beaten Romania. Everyone was celebrating after the match. My young fellow came in and put on a chip pan. Everything went on fire: the ceiling, the windows and everything else.

I tried to put out the fire. The oil splashed up on top of me. I was burned on my hands, face, legs, back and neck. My feet were badly cut after I walked on broken glass in the kitchen. Eventually, the fire brigade came to put the fire out. I was taken to hospital by ambulance and was kept in Intensive Care for three weeks.

I was very sick in hospital. The burns were very bad and I was heavily bandaged. I was very sore and had a lot of scabs from the burns. I was so bad that the relics of Padre Pio were brought in to me and I kept them on the table beside me. I also prayed to him at the time.

One evening, at about eight o'clock or nine o'clock, I was lying in my hospital bed. I was wide awake, in a big room, with a wall opposite me. It was a typical summer's evening and I was on my own. Suddenly, these strange pictures started coming up on the wall. It was like a slideshow. They were black-and-white pictures, lasting in all for about five minutes.

There was a picture of a hospital, a church, a town, the Stations of the Cross and mountains. After each picture, I could see steps. They were just ordinary steps, but were about 18 inches high. I would see a step, followed by a picture, followed by a step, followed by the next picture and so on. It was amazing.

I didn't know what the slides were about. There was no human being in them and certainly no Padre Pio. All I can remember is that there was great quietness and peace around me. I remember telling the woman who brought in the relics what had happened and what I had seen. She said, 'What you saw was San Giovanni. You should go out there and see for yourself.' I was surprised, as I had never even seen pictures of the place.

Eventually, I got better. I healed pretty well, although it took me months to recover. I was told by the consultant that I was lucky I didn't smoke or drink and my healing process was quite good as a result. However, I still have the scars to this day. My arms, hands, top of my head and back are still marked.

The following year, 1991, I went out on pilgrimage to San Giovanni. It was amazing when I got there. I saw everything I had seen in the slides. I saw the hospital. I saw the town, the church, the Stations of the Cross and the Gargano Mountains. They were exactly the same as I saw in the slides the year before. I could recognise them all.

I also saw the steps I had seen in the slides. They were the steps up to where he lived. Padre Pio used to go in the back way and he would climb up these steps. They were about 18 inches high, the same height as the ones I had seen. I had never known about them before, nor had I seen any of the other sights I saw while in hospital.

When I was there, I also had the great privilege of giving out communion in the crypt where Padre Pio is buried. When I was asked to do it, the group I was with said, 'You can't do that. Only priests can give out communion.' But I did it and I gave out communion in the crypt. I also went to confession with Fr. Alessio. I told him about what had happened to me and what I had seen. I told him I was still marked and I showed him the burns. He said, 'You have your own stigmata!' I found what he said very moving.

Middle Years

Looking back, I think Padre Pio came to me when I was in hospital and helped me to recover. I think he also showed me San Giovanni and sent me there. I eventually read the book *Padre Pio: The Irish Connection* and saw that, back in the 1970s, Fr. Alessio went around Ireland with slides which he showed to people at prayer meetings. They were the slides I saw in 1990.

I believe Padre Pio comes to people. He especially comes to those who are suffering. He is a great saint and a great healer. He certainly came to me; I'm sure of that. And I'm sure he healed me. But he also works in very strange ways, as I later discovered.

In 2011, my wife died. She had great devotion to Padre Pio, mainly as a result of what had happened to me in 1990. Eventually, I decided to put her photograph up on the wall in the sitting-room. But there was a problem doing that as there already was a photo on the wall, which was of Padre Pio. I decided to take it down.

I took Padre Pio's photo down and put it elsewhere. I left it upstairs, in a cupboard. Two hours later, I got a phone call to say you were looking for me to talk about what had happened to me and about Padre Pio. I ran up the stairs and brought Padre Pio's photo down straight away! He's now back on the wall where he was and that's where he'll stay!

ALAN, FROM COUNTY LIMERICK, outlines Padre Pio's role in his recovery from injuries sustained in two accidents.

In 1993, when I was about 18 years of age, I was at a bonfire which was lit to celebrate the winning of a sporting event. There were lots of people there. I ended up trying to jump over the fire. There was a big log burning in the middle of it.

As I jumped, I would put my leg on the log and use the log as leverage to jump the rest of it.

The problem was that the log was burning away. The last time that I jumped, the log snapped. My foot went into the fire and I fell down flat. I put my left hand out in front of me and saved my face, which never got burned. I then rolled out of the fire.

I burned my hand very badly. There was literally a hole in my palm and you could actually see into the hand. Melted tyre had burned into the skin. The burn was very painful and sore. I was taken to the local hospital and they said, 'We're sending you to Cork for skin grafts.'

There was a local woman in Limerick who was big into Padre Pio and she came and blessed me with one of his relics. I can't remember what the relic was. She prayed over my hand and she also gave me leaflets with prayers to say, which I still have to this day. That was my first introduction to Padre Pio.

A day or two after being blessed, a nurse took off the dressing and asked me, 'Why are you here? What are you in for?' She couldn't believe how good the hand looked. Another nurse was amazed, too. The hand was still red and raw, but the skin was back and there was no need to go to Cork for skin grafts. The doctors said, 'Off you go,' and they sent me home.

If you look at my hand now, you would say there was nothing wrong with it. I'm not badly scarred at all. There are just two black marks there, from the melted tyres, which look like black dirt. You might just think the marks were caused by a little bit of dirt on my hand. Where the hole in the hand was, there's no scar whatsoever.

At the time, I was only 18 years of age and I didn't think

that a miracle had happened. I was brought up to be a good Catholic and my parents believed you should go to Mass on a Sunday. However, I didn't become any more religious after what took place, although I did ask, 'How can you have a hole in the hand and two days later there's no hole in the hand?'

I was in deep trouble again on 29 April 2011. I was in my mid-30s at the time. I was working away up on the roof of a warehouse, fixing a hole in the roof. There were three of us there: one being a very good friend and the other a foreign lad who worked with us. I can remember telling the foreign lad to get in a little bit on the roof or he might go through it. I have no recollection of what happened after that. The rest is a blur.

It was a nice day, not wet or anything, although it may have been a bit windy, but weather wasn't the issue. Seemingly, from what I am told, I fell through the roof. We were walking off the roof, heading down for lunch. One of the lads, the foreign guy, was already gone. My friend was ahead of me and he heard a crash. He looked back and I was gone. I had fallen right through the roof.

I fell about 20 or 30 feet, they told me later. I believe I must have hit something on the way down and I landed on a concrete floor. I fractured my skull on the right-hand side, causing tinnitus, deafness and vertigo. I also seriously fractured my skull on the left-hand side, smashed my ribs and my collarbone, broke my cheekbone and a bone in my back, and I punctured my two lungs.

Although I don't remember a thing, my friends called an ambulance. They told me later that I was conscious and saying, 'I'm sorry! I'm sorry!' The ambulance brought me to hospital and they took me, later that day, down to Cork. I was in and out of an induced coma after that for about three weeks. At one stage, a clot blocked my ventilator and they nearly lost me. I was in a critical state, in Intensive Care, although I don't remember one bit of it.

My aunt-in-law came down to Cork, within the first week, and she was sitting in the hospital waiting-room. She spotted this man coming in who had a relic of Padre Pio. He was arriving to see someone else. She might have known him from before, I don't know. Anyhow, she asked him to go in and bless me. He said, 'Yes, of course I will.' So he came in and he blessed me with a Padre Pio relic.

A day or two later, the woman from Limerick who had blessed me at the time of the bonfire accident came to visit as well. She had heard that I was in big trouble again. She brought a first-class relic with her, she later told me, and she blessed me with it. It was brilliant what she did. I have to take my hat off to her for doing it, although again I don't remember one bit of it.

I think I was about a month in Cork and, afterwards, I was another month in hospital in Limerick. I was still so bad that I don't remember leaving there and coming back. My first real memory of that time was at the end of May when Manchester United played Barcelona in the Champions League final. I remember watching it on TV and United lost. I can recall being in hospital for that. Part of me was saying, 'Why am I here? Can I go home?' I didn't realise how bad I was.

I had fallen away and lost loads of weight. The first time I got on the weighing scales, I was under nine stone and I had been 16 or 17 stone. I had to have rehab, including physiotherapy and occupational therapy. Eventually, however, I improved a lot. I can walk and talk now, although I still have sore bones and sore ribs and a problem with my right ear. It was a slow process, but I slowly came back. I'm brilliant today, even though I'll never be back to where I was.

Looking back, I was extraordinarily lucky. I know of one person who fell four feet and he will be in a wheelchair for the rest of his life. Another person I know fell ten feet and he's in a wheelchair and can't talk. Yet I fell between 20 and 30 feet and I'm fine. People who saw me after the accident can't believe how well I look now.

Regarding my hand, I really don't know if Padre Pio cured it. You can believe it was either a miracle or that I had the best healing power known to man. However, I don't think even the doctors would believe my hand could have cured that well after two days. And the woman who brought the relic regarding my hand is a firm believer that it worked. Definitely, something strange happened and the evidence is very strongly in favour of Padre Pio.

Certainly, if I was in trouble in the future, I'd like to be blessed again. If my family was in trouble, I'd like them to be blessed, too. The reason is simple: I was in trouble twice and I got out of trouble twice and Padre Pio was the sole common denominator. His relics were involved in both cases and I came out of them. That's two out of two, which sounds like more than a coincidence. I feel I must have been blessed by him.

GEMMA, FROM COUNTY MEATH, describes how her ageing mother slept through a burglary, thanks to Padre Pio. It happened around 1994.

My mother, who was in her 80s, was living in Dublin at the time. Her husband had died over 30 years earlier and she had been on her own as a result. Her two children had moved away. However, she liked being in her own place. She was very bright and alert and her last job every night was to read the newspaper from cover to cover. She was very interested in current affairs and watched television. She was completely independent.

She was living in a safe place, with semi-detached houses and good neighbours around her. There were lots of houses there and she knew everybody. One particular neighbour would pop in and out and she would call me if my mother was unwell or anything like that. There were no burglaries or other worrying incidents.

At that time, my mother was a big devotee of Padre Pio. Her devotion stretched back to the early 1970s. Apparently, my aunt had met somebody who had a mitten of Padre Pio and, one night, my mother was invited to go along to prayers in the person's house. After that, my mother read about him and her devotion took off from there. She prayed to him every night and he was very important to her.

Her devotion was very simple. She felt that Padre Pio was a wonderful man and had great influence with the Lord. She was very impressed with his life and read most of the books which were around at the time. She would talk to him a lot, as if he were a friend. She always felt that if he was there, nothing could happen. She had great trust in him. In many ways, because my father wasn't around, she relied on Padre Pio to keep her safe.

One particular time, around 1994, my mother's next-door neighbours told her they were going away on holidays for a week or so. They dropped in their key, in case any member of their family came and wanted to get in. My mother didn't have any problem with that, as there were other neighbours close by. She wasn't worried at all.

MIDDLE YEARS

One night, while the neighbours were away, my mother locked up and went to bed in her bedroom upstairs, at the back of the house. She read the paper as usual and said her prayers. It was 11 o'clock or thereabouts. However, at around one o'clock or two o'clock in the morning, she woke up.

She had been woken by sounds coming from next-door. At first, she heard noise outside and then she thought she heard a door bang. She felt, 'That's funny! Maybe the neighbours are back.' She wondered if they had returned early from their holidays. As a result, she wasn't alarmed.

Just after that, she heard the sound of glass breaking in the kitchen, under where she was sleeping. She then heard the shuffling sound of people. Although she didn't hear voices, she knew there was somebody there. Soon, she heard another noise in the hallway and she thought, 'There's somebody downstairs!' She was clearly aware that there were people in the house. She asked herself, 'What will I do now?'

At that moment, she looked over into the corner of the bedroom, by the fireplace, and she saw Padre Pio. He was standing there quite clearly, with his hand raised. He was standing in light and had a kindly expression on his face. Straight away, he communicated to her, 'You have no problem, no worries, everything is going to be OK!'

Later on, I asked her, 'What did you do then?' She said, 'Well, I just lay down, turned around and faced the wall that is away from the door. I then fell asleep.' I don't think she even pulled the blankets up over her head; she just turned towards the wall and went to sleep. She trusted him that much; there wasn't a shadow of a doubt in her mind that she was going to be OK.

My mother slept right through the night. When she woke

up in the morning, she went out to have a look. Apparently, she had left something across the stair rail the night before, a blanket or something. That had fallen down the stairs, so she knew that someone had been upstairs. She then went downstairs and found that the house had been burgled.

They had taken a stereo and had gone through a sideboard looking for money. She also discovered that they had broken the glass on the back door and that's how they had come in. They had left the door wide open. After that, she just rang my brother and asked if he could come and fix a pane of glass. She never even said what the reason was. It was only when he arrived that what happened became evident.

She rang me that night and told me she had a burglary the night before. Needless to say, I nearly climbed a wall. I said, 'That's it, you've got to leave your home and come and live with us. You need somebody to be with you.' I went up the following day and made the house secure and brought her to live with us.

Looking back, she was really so calm around that event. She always had a great confidence that she wasn't alone. She matter-of-factly knew that Padre Pio had come to her and was over in the corner of her bedroom. It wasn't any big deal; she just expected it. Her faith was so strong in him that she knew he was looking after her. She retained that faith until her death in 1996.

A strange thing happened before she died. One night, she had a big haemorrhage. The next day, her breathing changed and they said, 'It won't be long now.' Although she had been unconscious, she suddenly opened up her eyes, sat up in the bed, fixed her gaze on the far corner of the room and a most beautiful smile lit up her face. She then lay back down in the bed and a minute later she died.

I think she must have seen my father at that moment before she died, but I really don't know who it was. It could have been Padre Pio. Either way, I know she has gone to meet him. And I know Padre Pio would have had his arms wide open waiting for her to arrive.

EILEEN, FROM COUNTY MAYO, reflects on how her tumour disappeared after she was blessed with a relic of Padre Pio.

As a young person, I didn't know about Padre Pio. I possibly had heard about him, but he didn't click with me. He didn't register. Eventually, when I was in my mid-30s, I heard about a novena to him and I went along to it. It was held on the first Monday of every month and it went on for nine months of the year. I became very loyal to it.

I had some problems in my family at the time. I found life was very difficult, but I discovered that praying to Padre Pio helped me. It brought me peace, comfort and hope. However, although I said the prayers and did the novenas, he didn't come alive for me until later.

I eventually had a road accident in 1995. A car came out from a side road and it crashed into me. It knocked me from side to side. My car was a write-off. I ended up with a very severe pain in my stomach. It was like my guts were being twisted, in the same way that you might twist a towel. The pain was very severe and it was very uncomfortable.

I remember going to a Padre Pio novena and I was so bad that I was doubled over with the pain. Afterwards, I had to walk a short distance and I was literally doubled over as I was walking along. I didn't know what it was, but I knew that something serious was wrong.

I ended up going into hospital and they decided to take my

appendix out. When I came home, I still had the same problem. I was still in bad pain and losing about one or two pounds of weight a week. I was all skin and bone. Eventually, I was taken for a barium enema scan and, afterwards, I got a phone call saying that they wanted me to come in for an operation.

I can recall the day that I went in; it was a beautiful day and the sun was shining. The consultant came and spoke to me. He said, 'Things aren't good. You have a tumour in your bowel. We need to operate and you'll probably have to wear a bag for the rest of your life.' He never told me anything more about the tumour; he just said it was there. He also told me it was a big operation. I sat there totally stunned.

After he left, I rang my husband and I also rang the priest who did the novena to Padre Pio. I left a message on his phone telling him what had happened. I said, 'I don't expect you to come up, but please remember me in your prayers and Masses.' The following evening, which was the day before the operation, he arrived up with a relic of Padre Pio.

I clearly remember him placing the relic on the area around my bowel. He blessed me and said, 'Keep praising Jesus and thanking him.' I got total peace and I accepted what was going to happen. I didn't know if I was going to live or die. I was worried about my husband and children, but regarding myself I felt, 'If it's God's will, I will accept it.'

The next day, on 7 June, I was taken down to theatre and had my operation. They removed a foot of my main bowel. They found that I had diverticulitis, which is a digestive disease involving the formation of little pockets within the bowel wall. It is pretty common and wouldn't have been the cause of my problems. But they found no tumour.

I was brought back to Intensive Care and was out of it,

with tubing coming out of me and all that. I asked one of the doctors if they had found the tumour. He said, 'The more we looked, the less we could see.' I was amazed and told him I had devotion to Padre Pio and had prayed to him and had been blessed with his relic before the operation. 'Well, it had to be something,' he said. 'My parents have great devotion to Padre Pio as well.'

The cancer was gone and I think what had happened was a miracle. My consultant later told my husband that he couldn't find the tumour and my husband felt that what had happened was a genuine miracle, too. Afterwards, I checked with my own doctor and he had heard about the tumour as well, so it had existed; he had been informed. Later, I also got to see the consultant's notes and twice he had written, 'No tumour found.'

After what happened, I gave my testimony at the Padre Pio weekend in Knock. My testimony was also published in *The Voice of Padre Pio* magazine, which comes out of San Giovanni. I have been to San Giovanni about ten or 11 times. And I try to promote Padre Pio as much as I possibly can by taking his relic around to people in hospital and other places.

I really feel I was given a second chance. I have never been sick since what happened, thank God. Every morning I wake up to the sound of the birds singing and I appreciate nature like never before. I feel overjoyed and I feel a great sense of peace. My faith is stronger and I have developed even greater devotion to Padre Pio. I feel he is looking after me. He has really come alive for me since what happened back in 1995.

ANNA, FROM CORK CITY, remembers how her voice problems were cured while on a visit to San Giovanni Rotondo.

On 17 August 1995, my husband and I were in Barleycove. We were there for a couple of days. When I was walking along the beach, I suddenly realised that my voice was gone. I had sometimes got a touch of laryngitis, but this was different. I couldn't speak; I was trying to, but I could only whisper. There was no strength in my voice; it was as if I was only miming. I was worried about what might be wrong.

My GP arranged an appointment with a specialist, so I went to him on 31 August and I explained everything as well as I could. There was enough strength in my voice for him to understand me. He sprayed an anaesthetic on my throat and examined it with a scope. He thought there was a nodule there, or something in that line. He told me that he would like to further examine me in hospital, under anaesthetic, and asked me to arrange with his secretary a time when I could go in.

Sometime previously, I'd had a much smaller medical problem and a friend of mine, who was a very good Padre Pio devotee, gave me a novena to say. I had prayed to him and everything was fine. It gave me the strength and the knowledge to realise that this was the person who could help me with my throat. I thought I would like to go to San Giovanni before I went into hospital.

I spoke to the secretary about an admission date and she was offering me one immediately, but I knew, at the time, that there was a pilgrimage going from Cork to San Giovanni from 17 – 24 September and I wanted to go on that. The secretary agreed that I could travel to San Giovanni first and she made a hospital appointment for shortly after my return, towards the end of September.

In San Giovanni, we went to Padre Pio's cell and I got this beautiful smell of roses. I was told that to get this 'odour of sanctity' is a sign that Padre Pio is looking after you. I got it a second time as well. It was a beautiful smell, not like anything that you would usually come in contact with. It wasn't like something you would smell in a chemist shop; it was just something special, a beautiful, natural smell.

I also went to a Mass celebrated by Fr. Joseph Pius. This was on the night of 22 September, down at the tomb, just before Padre Pio's feast day the following day. Fr. Joseph Pius celebrated the Mass and gave me communion. He looked at me in a very spiritual way, as if he was asking for something or indicating that I was going to be granted something. I felt there was something very saintly about him. That, and the smell of roses, gave me confidence that I would be cured.

That night, I was going to go to the vigil, but the heavens opened and we couldn't go out as planned. Instead, we were all sitting around in the foyer of the hotel. Most of those on the pilgrimage were there, too. I was trying to talk or, more correctly, to whisper. I was sitting on a couch between two ladies. Our courier was on one side and another lady, from Tullamore, was on the other. I was just chatting to the two of them.

I was trying to say something when, the next thing, my voice came back. I think I was trying to answer in a whisper, but my full voice came out. I could suddenly hear it. I was amazed. Everybody else was amazed, too. People said, 'She's talking!' Everybody was around me, flabbergasted and, of course, relieved and happy.

Before that, throughout the pilgrimage, I was only able to whisper. There was no real sound, just a gush of air. All that week, I had been saying, 'Please, God, I ask that my voice will come back again.' However, at that stage, I was also wondering, 'Am I ever going to get any relief?' After it returned, I felt, 'Thanks be to God!'

What a relief it was. There were celebrations and drinks all round. Although I had got a shock, I felt great. I just talked and talked that night; you couldn't stop me. I met some of those people along the way afterwards and they would always come to me and say how they were so delighted by what happened in San Giovanni. I knew it was the power of the Lord.

That night, I had a dream which felt very real. I could see angels ascending to heaven and I saw the robe of a Capuchin, which was also going up. Although I couldn't see a face or a head with the robe, I felt it was definitely Padre Pio going up with his angels, heading back to heaven. The following morning, I went to thank the Lord at Mass for what he had done.

We eventually came back to Ireland. I went to my GP first and he said, 'Faith is a wonderful thing.' I then went into hospital for my appointment with the specialist. He examined me under anaesthetic. He came to tell me afterwards, 'There is nothing there. Everything is fine.'

What happened did a lot for my faith. I went back to San Giovanni the next year and took my sister with me. She, too, got the beautiful smell of roses. I was over for Padre Pio's beatification and canonisation. I think the beatification meant more to me, although I will never forget the canonisation because it was so warm that day they had to spray water around. I haven't been there since because of my age; somebody would have to look after me and I would spoil their visit.

I think Padre Pio is just wonderful. Every day, I say the same prayers that he used to say. I pray to Our Lady as well. I also pray to St. Joseph because Padre Pio was very fond of him. I think Padre Pio brought about my cure, through the power of God. God is all-powerful and Padre Pio asked him to cure me. It was granted to him because he was special in the eyes of the Lord. He did what I had pleaded with him to do and I think he was glad he had done it.

FR. TOM, WHO COMES ORIGINALLY FROM COUNTY KILKENNY but who currently lives in County Laois, explains how he developed his devotion to Padre Pio.

I was ordained as a priest in 1966, but there was no room for me in my diocese as the place was chock-a-block with priests that year. I was told to find myself a posting abroad. I ended up in Australia and was sent to an outpost where there was no electricity or running water or anything else. I was out beyond the rabbit-proof fence and I worked with Maori sheepshearers.

One day, a two-seater, light plane landed in a field and this white man, in his mid-60s, got out. I was sent to talk to him. He had run out of aviation fuel and he said, 'Can you help?' We were 200 or 300 miles from a petrol station, so I replied, 'We might be able to do something for you by tomorrow evening, but in the meantime you are welcome to stay the night.'

We sat around the fire that night and I said to him, 'What do you do?' He said, 'I'm a bishop.' I said, 'What? I'm the Pope!' It took him two hours to convince me he was a bishop and it took me another two hours to convince him I was a priest. I told him what I was doing there and he said, 'I'm starting a mission in India and Pakistan, setting up schools for the poor. Would you like to go?' So that's where I ended up.

I spent most of my time in India, with just a little time in Pakistan. In India, there was no food and I neglected myself. I went down to seven stone in weight. I came home to Ireland to get myself rectified and the bishop wouldn't let me go back. That was back in March 1998, 32 years after I had left for the missions.

I was given a posting to Kilkenny, where I loved caring for the elderly and the not so well-off. I'd look after them and bring them communion every day. One day, I met an old man, who was aged 94, and I cared for him for about six months. Every time I would go into his room, there was this statue there. I didn't want to show my ignorance by saying, 'Who's your man?' I didn't know of Padre Pio at the time.

One morning, the man leaned over and handed me the statue. He said, 'You take that, because I'm nearly finished in this life. That statue will be powerful in your hands.' I said, 'Who is he?' He didn't show any surprise that I didn't know and he replied, 'Padre Pio.' He then spoke to me about Padre Pio in a very loving way. I was converted on the spot.

I treasured that statue from then on because of the way it was given to me. I think the man died the very day he handed it to me and I always remember his words, 'That statue will be powerful in your hands.' Soon, I was talking to other people about Padre Pio and they were saying, 'Yeah, yeah, we pray to him all the time.' Every second person I met seemed to be his friend.

After that, I took to Padre Pio like a duck to water and he took to me, too, I hope. I think what appealed to me about him was his humility and his sanctity. He always had great time for the Sacred Heart and Our Lady, as I did. His stigmata got to me, too. How could a person be so holy? I often said to myself, 'I wish to God I could be that holy and I could take the pain of the stigmata.' I was also impressed by how he had said Mass.

People soon started coming to me with their problems and looking for the statue. I would ask them, 'How did you know about me?' Without exception, they would say, 'Somebody told me,' nothing else. Two of the first people who arrived were women in their 20s with breast cancer, who had come all the way from County Cork. I asked them, 'How did you hear about me?' They said, 'Somebody told us.' I began to put two and two together and I felt, 'Padre Pio is doing this.'

Soon, a lot of children were being brought to me or I was being asked to pray for them, and there were many successes. I can think of a recent one involving a 12-year-old whose neck was thought to be broken after an accident playing soccer. That night, I prayed to Padre Pio on my knees beside my bed. I had a list of people to pray for and this young lad was top of the list.

I always say to people, 'Leave it with Padre Pio. Have faith in him and get some sleep.' That night, however, I couldn't sleep a wink. I kept waking up and thinking of Padre Pio. I also had a dream where I was coming out of the hospital with the young lad and there were reporters and cameras there. I remember saying to them, 'Prayer! Prayer! Prayer! Pray to Padre Pio and you will be alright!' The next day, I got word from the child's mother saying the MRI scan showed that the neck wasn't broken.

There was also a four-year-old child who was diagnosed with leukaemia. I prayed to Padre Pio and got the family praying as well. The child was going up to Dublin every week for chemotherapy and was in a bad way. The mother had to leave her job to look after her.

I remember one Sunday, just before Christmas, the mother and child were in the back of the church and it was cold. The child had lost her hair and was wearing a beanie. Her younger sister jumped up into my arms and was talking to me. She said, 'Fr. Tom, aren't those roses something special?' I couldn't smell any roses, but the child could.

The mother said, 'Stop talking nonsense. It's Christmastime and there are no roses.' The girl started to cry and said, 'But it's all around us.' I began to go weak at the knees. I thought, 'Padre Pio is here!' I put my hand on the head of the child who was wearing the beanie and the beanie stuck to my hand. When I pulled it away, the beanie came with it. I thought, 'Padre Pio is telling us something!'

The mother then said she was going up to Dublin the next day. I said, 'Give me a ring when you're up there.' I don't know why I said that, but I really felt something was going to happen. And it did. They did the usual tests at the hospital the next day and the specialist said to the mother, 'There's no leukaemia in that child!' The child was fine.

Another example involved grandparents who came to me about their grandchild who was very ill in hospital. The child wasn't expected to live and the family were worried stiff. The grandparents asked me to pray to Padre Pio. I had little relics and I gave them one. I said, 'Put that under the child's pillow and say a prayer to Padre Pio,' and that's what they did. The next morning, at about eight o'clock, the child woke up and said, 'Mammy, I'm hungry,' and that child was fine.

I certainly think that Padre Pio is a miracle worker, no two

Middle Years

ways about it. I have seen that for myself. I could spend hours giving you examples, especially relating to children, with doctors saying, 'How did this happen?' I love helping children and Padre Pio loved them, too. When I pray for a child who is sick or who is dying, I really mean it. Maybe that's why things happen.

I keep saying to people to ask Padre Pio for help. I say, 'Ask him and leave it to him, then back off. Have faith in him.' I tell them, 'When you go to bed tonight, visualise Padre Pio in the furthest corner of your room. Tell him your problem and then fall asleep. If you have enough faith in him, you will be able to do that.' I also tell them that that sort of faith didn't come to me overnight; I had to work at it.

You have to believe totally and trust implicitly. The more I read about him, I think he does need your 100 per cent faith. There's no 99 per cent with Padre Pio. If you have that faith, he will answer your prayers in his way, if it's the will of God, as my mother used to always say. He will never refuse you.

KATHRYN, FROM COUNTY GALWAY, attributes her revival from a brain haemorrhage to the intercession of Padre Pio.

I was at work back in 1999 when I got this ferocious headache, which came on quite suddenly. It went from just being a light headache to my crawling on the floor trying to get relief. I felt nauseous and was trying to get sick, but couldn't do so. I knew there was something major going on. I had never had headaches before and had experienced nothing like this.

I went to the hospital, where they thought I had migraine, yet they agreed to keep me in overnight. As we found out later, I had just had a brain haemorrhage. After that, I don't remember very much. I was just coming and going and was basically out of it. I did, however, have a second bleed that night. They scanned me and found that there were two bleeds going on.

I knew that I was very close to dying. I couldn't feel with my right hand and I couldn't see. Instead, I could only feel with my left hand. I also remember there was this wonderful nurse there who stayed with me through the night. She never left my side. I didn't want to die without my husband being there, holding my hand, but it was night-time and, in his place, she held my hand. She never let it go until he came and took over.

I remember waking up early in the morning, at 7.20, and the doctor arrived to tell me there were two bleeds on the brain. Right behind him was a priest, who had arrived to anoint me. It was like they were queuing up. I thought, 'My God! I'm in trouble here!' I wanted to see my kids, who were young, but I didn't get to do so because I was quickly ferried off by ambulance to Dublin.

I remember lying on the flat of my back in the ambulance and trying to remember the Our Father. I could start it, but I couldn't remember the words and I couldn't finish it. I was also looking up at this oval-shaped glass on the ambulance ceiling, while trying to figure out where we were on the road. The driver got me to Dublin in only two hours and ten minutes, which was very fast for those days.

I was immediately rushed to the High Dependency Unit. I was constantly throwing up and I was coming and going and coming and going. A doctor came in and asked me questions. I knew what I wanted to say, but I couldn't get it out of my mouth. I became very bad, very low, and I actually wanted to die with the pain. I didn't care. I felt so ill. I just wanted to get away from the pain.

Middle Years

It was extremely busy in High Dependency. I remember there was a man in there who was with his wife and she had been through surgery. She was in a coma and was expected to die. There were only the two of them; they had no children. He looked over at my husband and saw him crying. He came over and he asked him, 'Are you Catholic?' My husband said, 'We are.' He replied, 'I don't know if it will do anything, but here's a relic of Padre Pio. Rub it on her head. You never know.'

My husband put it on my head and started to say the Our Father. He didn't even get halfway through it when I shot up in the bed and I started violently throwing up. The darkest green bile came out of my stomach. I threw up and threw up. There were little cardboard dishes there and my husband couldn't find enough of them, or keep them coming fast enough, to catch the flow. Every time I threw up, I would shoot up in the bed and vomit, and it felt like I was relieving the pressure in my brain. It was as if I was being kept alive somehow.

Around that time, I also asked my husband if he could get in touch with a man down in Cork who had Padre Pio relics. I had met him in Medjugorje in the mid-1980s. I felt, 'It's the only hope I have.' My husband found his number and called him. He flew up immediately and brought with him a glass cross with a relic of Padre Pio in it.

He came into the ward and all I remember him saying was, 'Ask your guardian angel to go in front of Our Lord to plead your case.' He said, 'He's the only one who can go in front of Our Lord and ask for help for you.' That's what I did and I felt I had some hope.

I then asked the man to bless everyone else in the room. He

did so, until there was one last man left: the man whose wife had given the relic to my husband. I don't know what their conversation consisted of, but afterwards the man said, 'Will you please thank your friend because I can now accept whatever the Lord sends. I can now let my wife go.'

I eventually stroked and they brought me for an MRI scan. I went straight from that into surgery. The surgeon said to my husband, 'We're going to have to operate and put in a little hole to relieve the pressure. There's a very strong possibility that she's not going to make it. The best-case scenario is that there's a ten per cent chance that she will survive. If she does survive, it's guaranteed that she's going to be in rehab to learn how to walk and talk again.'

The surgeon said the operation would take about an hour or an hour-and-a-quarter. Five-and-a-half or six hours later, I still hadn't reappeared. I don't really know what had happened. My husband said, after I came out, that I informed him I loved him. He said, 'She's fine. She's grand.' I was hallucinating a lot after that, but two days later I insisted on getting up and washing my hair. They had shaved half my head and left the other half, and I wanted to wash it.

The nurse went ballistic. The doctor came in and the nurse was still giving out stink. He looked at her and said, 'Look around. This is the nearest thing to a miracle. First of all, there was only a ten per cent chance she was going to survive, but she's talking and walking. Let the woman do what she wants.' He also said, 'Look at everybody else.' All the others were not in a good state. That was the first sign I was coming back and it was only 48 hours after the operation.

All I can tell you is that I believe every single one of us in High Dependency walked out of there, and I wasn't even the worst of them. I know that the wife of the man who gave my husband the relic was still alive all the time I was there and I was there for a month. For months afterwards, we watched the papers for her death, but it never appeared. And she certainly didn't die while I was there. It seems we all survived. All of us were blessed by the man from Cork and I have no doubt what happened.

I am definite I was saved by Padre Pio. That day when I vomited after the relic was put on me, I know it took the pressure off my head. I also believe the man from Cork was destined to come up not just to help me but to bless everybody else as well. In addition, I have often wondered, 'Why was I kept alive?' A lot of what I have done since then has concerned health and wellness and I think my role on this earth is to help people with their physical bodies. That's what I do to this day.

I also have no doubt that God really does exist and he's working for us all the time. I'm not one of those people who rush up to the altar every five minutes. But I believe in God. I believe that God is love. And I believe in Padre Pio. I have absolutely no doubt about what he did for me.

PATRICIA, FROM COUNTY CORK, talks about Padre Pio's role in her son's battle with cancer throughout most of 1999.

My son Keith was a 14-year-old, perfectly healthy boy who found it easy to make friends. He had a bubbly personality. He started complaining of headaches, so we took him to the doctor, who thought that it might be a touch of migraine. However, a few weeks later, he got a very bad attack and he was rushed to hospital. It turned out that he had secondary cancer in the brain.

He was taken to Dublin by ambulance and we were told

that he would only have a few days before he would die. It was diagnosed that he had testicular cancer. The tumour was only half the size of a pea, yet it had spread to his lungs and up into his head. It was everywhere. He was covered in cancer and there was no hope.

Although he was diagnosed with cancer, he was very good dealing with it. He was phoning his friends from school and saying, 'Guys, guess what I have? I've got cancer.' He was very positive, great to look after, a very good patient and he never complained.

He started to get treatment, including chemotherapy and radiotherapy, because the doctor said that at least it would shrink the tumours and that he would get longer to live. He became very sick. All his hair fell out and he got very thin. Throughout it, we were up and down between Cork and Dublin, as he would be let home for a few days. He would be so nauseated during the drive that you would have to stop the car on occasions and he would always be apologising. He was a beautiful boy.

All of the time, I asked Padre Pio to help us. I had heard about him through my mum, who had great love for him. She always talked about him and she brought all of us over to San Giovanni on different occasions. All she ever wanted for Christmas was money for Padre Pio, because he was always building something. She was a big devotee, although my dad wasn't.

She and my dad went over to San Giovanni to visit him. They went to his Masses in the morning. My dad met Padre Pio and kissed his wounds; women weren't allowed to do it at the time. The first time my mum saw Padre Pio, she got the smell of narcissi and, when she was getting on the plane and

Middle Years

leaving, she got the same incredible smell. Apparently, that was the way he used to say goodbye.

When Keith was sick, I got leaflets containing prayers to Padre Pio and I used to say them all the time. I would ask, 'Padre Pio, please look after Keith and protect him and bring him a cure.' I always had this great peace and this great feeling that he was going to be fine. I was very confident that God was going to cure him.

At the back of my mind, however, I must have been aware that he wasn't going to live, because I would always add, 'Padre Pio, if Keith can't live, please let him do his purgatory here on earth so that I can be with him and help him with it.' I suppose I thought doing his purgatory here on earth would get him quicker to heaven if he died. I think that's what he did – his purgatory – throughout his illness.

I also had Padre Pio relics brought to Keith and he was blessed with them. The mitten was brought to him, together with one of the bandages. A woman, who had met Padre Pio and had a lock of his hair in a special locket, gave it to my sister-in-law and she was always bringing it in. It was a lock of Padre Pio's grey hair. On several nights, Keith used to wear the locket around him.

After Keith was finally discharged from hospital, we were told that there was no hope, although I still clung on to the belief that he would live. We brought him home and, on Christmas Eve 1999, he was very, very sick. He couldn't walk and he was in a wheelchair. That afternoon, on Christmas Eve, I remember sitting beside his bed and I said, 'OK, Lord, if he can't live, I'd like you to take him as soon as possible because I don't want him to suffer any more.' He died on Christmas Day.

It was very special that he passed away on Christmas Day. For me, it was such a beautiful gift. I have sometimes read that people who die on Christmas Day go straight to heaven. It's one of the days that heaven's gates are opened. The Lord was telling me he went straight to him and it made my grieving so much easier. Throughout the funeral, I was thinking, 'Keith, you're so lucky, go now and enjoy it,' because he had suffered so much.

I did question why Keith had to die and why things had to be so hard. I asked, 'Why didn't you let him live?' But I think Keith has been spared a lot in this world. Everybody suffers in life and he's been spared that. I know he suffered near the end, but now he is in heaven and I would much rather him to be with the Lord than here. Even though I miss him, I know he wouldn't want to come back. He's in a happier place.

What happened totally changed my life. I thought I knew the Lord, but I only prayed to keep in with him. I'm also nowhere near as materialistic as I was. It's like a light was shone on my soul. The Lord's my rock now. He's my reason for living. I also still have devotion to Padre Pio and I regard him as a very kind priest and a saint who helped me in my hour of need.

LATER YEARS

On 20 January 2000, a seven-year-old Italian boy named Matteo Colella developed a very high fever while at school. Further symptoms appeared later on in the day, including vomiting, lethargy and strange-looking spots. Residing in San Giovanni Rotondo, where his father worked as a doctor, Matteo was rushed to the local hospital and admitted to Intensive Care.

Things soon took a turn for the worst. Problems arose with his heart and his lungs and he went into a state of shock. A pulmonary oedema caused foam to spill from his mouth. He was diagnosed as having hyper-acute meningitis with multi-organ failure. Doctors felt there was nothing they could do and believed that the young boy was lost.

Matteo's mother, Maria Lucia, threw herself at the mercy of Padre Pio. She sought, and received, permission to pray by Padre Pio's bed at the monastery in San Giovanni and also at the granite stone covering his remains. She prayed for many days, always recalling the friar's words, 'Prayer is a powerful weapon, a key which opens the heart of God.'

Despite the bleak prognosis, Matteo Colella recovered and was eventually discharged from hospital. He later explained to his mother how, while comatose, he was visited by what he described as 'an old man, with a white beard.' The man said, 'Don't worry, you will get better soon.' On being shown an image of Padre Pio, Matteo said, 'It is him.....it was Padre Pio who was with me!'

The revival of Matteo Colella was later declared by the Congregation for the Causes of Saints to be a miracle, having first been pronounced by a medical panel to be scientifically inexplicable. As a result, Padre Pio was canonised by Pope John Paul II, in the presence of more than 300,000 people, on 16 June 2002.

In many ways, the canonisation marked the high point of Irish devotion to Padre Pio, with some 4,000 travelling over to Rome for the ceremony. In subsequent years, although the excitement had diminished, devotion continued. Irish prayer groups remained active and demand for his relics, especially by the sick, remained high. More tellingly, perhaps, Padre Pio copper-fastened his standing as Ireland's favourite saint.

BRIAN, FROM CORK, describes how his brother miraculously recovered from a mysterious illness.

In 2001, my two brothers and I had just come home from secondary school when one of them collapsed in the middle of the kitchen floor. He didn't become unconscious, but he seemed very fazed. He was 15 at the time and I was 17. It had been a normal day and we were still in our school uniforms. We were just in the door. It was around 4.30 or 4.45 in the afternoon.

My brother was like that on the ground for probably ten minutes. I didn't know what to do. Because he was always up to devilment, the first thing that came to my mind and my other brother's mind was, 'He's after getting into trouble with a teacher and he's trying to deflect attention.' However, after about ten minutes, we could see it was very serious. His face had gone as white as a ghost. He looked very bad.

LATER YEARS

We got him into the car and my mother, who had been at home, drove him straight to the hospital. My father met them there. The doctors examined him, but they couldn't find anything wrong. They did test after test after test. They eventually narrowed it down to a kind of a brain virus, but they could never fully establish what it was and they could never identify a cure.

For the next three years, my brother got sicker and sicker and sicker. His life became very difficult. He was confined to a wheelchair for a time. He lost the use of his legs for about three months and he became like a skeleton. His body was so weak that he was eventually confined to bed. He even had to be anointed because we all expected him to go. My mother was at her wit's end.

Eventually, a neighbour mentioned to my mother, 'There's this guy called Donald Enright, who has a Padre Pio glove. It's very powerful and you should pray with it.' My mother rang him and he said he would bring it to the house. We weren't overly-religious at the time, although we went to Mass every Sunday. We also had no particular devotion to Padre Pio, even though we had some images of him around the house. They came from my aunt, who was a nun over in England, and she would send us cards or other little things relating to Padre Pio.

Donald Enright came on Easter Saturday and went into my brother's room, along with my mother and father. He prayed there and put the Padre Pio glove under my brother's head. He left it there as my brother drifted off to sleep. Donald said to my mother, 'That's a very, very sick boy.' He also said something like, 'It will take a miracle to get him better.'

The following day, we were all in the kitchen with the exception of my brother, who was in his bedroom close by. The next thing, we heard a roar from the bedroom. My brother was calling out for my mother. I thought he might have fallen. My mother ran straight in and I followed immediately after her.

What we saw was amazing. My brother was at the side of his bed, standing and using his legs. He was in total shock and saying, 'Look! Look! Look at my legs!' He was taking baby steps. My mother was speechless. She was trying to talk, but she couldn't. She started crying with relief and happiness. It was a very big moment. What we saw was as good as if my brother was dancing across the room.

From that day onwards, my brother started getting stronger and stronger and he started coming out of it. He had been getting blinding pains out through his eyes, but they eventually started decreasing. He started moving his legs. His health came back and the colour came back into his cheeks. The doctors were totally baffled and couldn't explain it.

He eventually got back to living an ordinary life. It took probably another year for a full recovery to happen, so he suffered for such a long time. Including the two years he was at his worst, it took three years in all. However, he eventually got his whole life back on track, he's getting on really well, and there's no doubt that the change occurred on that Easter Saturday.

I am 100 per cent convinced that what took place was a miracle. Without a doubt, I believe that it was due to the intercession of Padre Pio. My brother also put it all totally down to him. As a result, our whole family developed a very strong devotion to the Rosary and to Our Lady. We started going to Mass regularly. Everything stemmed back to that day when the glove was brought to my brother.

Looking back on it now, that was the start of a big interest for me in my faith. What happened blew me away. I felt I had seen a miracle with my own eyes. Although I had been going to Mass on a Sunday, I was doing it more out of habit than anything else. There was no personal relationship there with the Lord or Our Lady, but that all changed.

I developed a big devotion to Padre Pio and I started saying the Rosary regularly. Although I went on to college, I kept up my devotion to him. I read about him a lot and was really impressed. I also developed a big devotion to Our Lady. It was a long process, but I am now in a seminary, studying for the priesthood.

Years ago, if someone had told me I would end up in a seminary, I would have laughed them out the door. But what took place was clearly meant to be and it was a gift from God through the intercession of Padre Pio. Of all the saints, he is someone I pray to every day and he's now a very important part of my life. What happened with my brother was the catalyst for all of that.

CHARLENE, FROM COUNTY DERRY, tells of her revival from a brain tumour, thanks to Padre Pio. The event dates back to 2003.

On the day before my eleventh birthday, I felt unwell. I was sick and had a sore head. I had been out playing, but I came in and told Mummy and Daddy how I felt. I had a lie-down and I ended up sleeping for a few hours. When I woke up, I felt just as bad. The left-hand side of my face had dropped. I couldn't open my left eye and my speech was quite slurred. I also had a very bad headache. It was most unusual as I was never really sick as a child.

My mummy and daddy took me for a check-up. After examining me, the doctors thought it might be a case of Bell's palsy, which is a form of facial paralysis. Although they were letting me go home, Mummy knew there wasn't something right, so she asked them to send me to the hospital, which they did.

At this stage, I was deteriorating. I was very spaced out and I wasn't interacting. Whenever someone asked me a question, it was taking me perhaps ten minutes to answer. The doctor did some tests and I wasn't responding. She noticed that my symptoms were on my left side, so she put a pen on my left side and said, 'Charlene, can you lift that pen?' I reached across with my right hand to lift it. She knew then that it had something to do with my brain.

They kept me in the hospital that night. I was in my own room because of the severity of what they thought was wrong with me. On the next day – my eleventh birthday – the nurses made me a cake. All my family and friends came in and were hugging me and giving me presents. Although I was drugged up, I was a bit more interactive and I can remember some things that happened. I can particularly remember the doctor coming in and taking my mummy and daddy away.

They came back about 20 or 30 minutes later. I noticed that their faces were blotchy and there were tears in their eyes. I knew something was wrong. They told me I had a brain tumour. As I was just 11, I didn't know what a brain tumour was and I was asking them about it. It turned out that the tumour was the size of a man's fist and was in the middle of my brain.

The doctors told my family to prepare for the worst. They even thought I might die that night. A priest came in to see me and he confirmed me. My whole family was there, along with my godparents. Then, because the hospital didn't have the facilities to care for me, I was driven by ambulance in the middle of the night to the children's hospital in Belfast.

After a day or two, a brain surgeon came in to see me. He sat down beside my bed. He said he had taken my files home the night before. He had talked to his wife about me and prayed and couldn't sleep. But he felt I had to be operated on and he believed he had something to offer me that others couldn't offer.

Apparently, nobody else felt that they could take my case on because of the severity of what was wrong. I had only a 20 per cent chance of survival. However, he said he was willing to take me on and would do the surgery. After that, I remained in the hospital until the operation was scheduled to take place.

Two nights before the operation, a man came in with the mitt of Padre Pio. My mummy and daddy had arranged for him to see me. I was lying down in my bed and my family were around me. There were lots of people there as I am the youngest of ten. Partners of my brothers and sisters were there, too. Some of my young friends had also come in to see me.

The man told me to lift my head up, as I was very weak at the time. I felt really tired and closed my eyes. Everyone then started saying the Rosary and prayed to Padre Pio to intercede for me. Although my eyes were still closed, I could feel this pressure at the top of my head. I wasn't sure what was causing it, but I thought it was the man pushing on my head. I didn't open my eyes, but I felt this pushing and pushing. There were tears coming out of my eyes and I also felt a sensation coming over my body, right down to my stomach.

The whole thing lasted probably about five minutes and then

the man left. I said to my mummy, 'Why was that man pushing so hard against my head?' She said, 'Charlene, he wasn't. He was with us at the bottom of the bed; there was no one at the top of the bed.' All we could think of was that the pressure I felt had something to do with Padre Pio.

Two days later, I had my operation. They had to open up my skull and the operation lasted eight-and-a-half hours. It was hard on me, but it was even harder on my family who didn't know what was going on. We later heard that they had removed most of the tumour. Only a very small fraction was left behind. They then analysed what they had taken out and it was benign!

They first told my mummy and daddy that it was benign and it was they who told me. We were all so relieved that it wasn't malignant. It also hadn't spread throughout my body. They additionally told us that what was left of the tumour would never change. They said it would never get smaller, but it would either stay the same or, God forbid, it might grow. However, contrary to what they said, the tumour has actually shrunk over time.

The doctors were astounded at how well everything had gone. They couldn't believe it. From the first night I entered hospital, they thought I wouldn't survive. After the operation, I even got home early. They expected me to be in hospital for a month at least; however, I was home six days later. So I really believe what happened was a miracle. I believe that wholeheartedly.

I am fine now and every day I wake up and I am so thankful. I just say, 'Thank you, Jesus.' Without him, I wouldn't be here. I believe that, through him, I was given a second chance in life. As a result, I am now devoted to my faith and I am so thankful for everything regarding my religious beliefs that my mummy and daddy, who are very humble, holy people, have passed down to me.

I also am devoted to Padre Pio. I pray to him every day. I pray through him all the time and I ask him to intercede. I don't necessarily say Our Fathers to him, although I do that, too. Mostly, I just talk to him in my head and I have a conversation with him. I ask him to remain close to me and hold my hand as I walk through life. And he has helped me in so many ways, it's unbelievable.

I have no doubt he interceded for me and looked after me. I think everything panned out the way it did because of him. I don't really know what happened and I don't think I'll ever know until I get to heaven. But something definitely happened and I believe I am here now because of the power of prayer and through his intercession. As a result, I love him dearly and regard him as a very good friend.

MARION, FROM COUNTY MAYO, witnessed a different type of Padre Pio miracle, which was experienced by a woman she once cared for.

I once worked as a home help. I wanted a job where I could take the children with me or be at home when they arrived in from school. I had two children and I felt that this type of work would suit. I put the word out about what I was looking for. Initially, I worked for a lady for a short period before she died. That lasted for about six months. She had to go into a nursing home and eventually passed away.

The district nurse then put me in touch with a lady called Annie. That would have been around the year 2000. She had a condition related to arthritis, which crippled her. She was stiff and in constant pain. She couldn't sleep because of the pain. She had very little mobility and would have to be helped out of bed or when she went to the bathroom. Her legs and the soles of her feet were completely ulcerated.

She was in real trouble. She couldn't make her bed or wash herself or do her hair or put on her shoes. She couldn't bend down. In the kitchen, she couldn't get to the bottom cupboard or reach over her head. She would even have difficulty peeling, as she couldn't hold the peeler. Eventually, she would be just sitting there and had to be fed.

Although she had four children, they were grown up and had moved away. Because of that, I would go to her house for maybe two hours a day, although I did more hours as time went on. I would do all the housework, the washing and the cleaning and keeping the fires going. It helped her a lot.

She had a husband, but he had some problems, too. He was a good bit older than she was and he had Alzheimer's. He got sicker and sicker. He would be very forgetful and he couldn't remember who Annie was or who he was. He might say about Annie, 'I can't get rid of that old woman who is here in the house.' When other people would visit, he might say to me, 'Let's get out of here. We don't want to be here with those old people.'

I would look after him, too. He didn't want to be in the house. I might take him out in the car, to give him a break. Yet, although he was in a bad way, she made sure that he was taken care of at home, even though she herself was in a dreadful state. He might have to be helped going to bed and she'd arrange that. She always loved him. She would say, 'I love him so much. He was such a kind man and he was so good to me.'

LATER YEARS

During all this time, Annie had great faith in Padre Pio and prayed to him a lot. She had a photograph of him in a brown frame, which she would bring from the bedroom into the kitchen or to wherever she was. It was like she was bringing a friend with her. She always carried it everywhere. She might have him on the mantelpiece or over the sink. At night, he'd be on the chest of drawers near her bed. When she'd wake up, he'd be the first thing she'd see.

Padre Pio was always on her mind. The sense of peace he brought her was just beautiful. Her face would be calm and serene and she was always smiling. She made it all seem so easy. She always had a positive word to say and never said anything unkind, no matter what happened. She always saw the bright side of things. It was a thing of great beauty and I would feel that it was something I should be working towards myself.

I remember, one day, I was with her and she had the Padre Pio magazine which she used to have sent to her. I think it was a Monday and the postman had just delivered it. She had it in her hand as I walked in. She pointed to a picture of Padre Pio in the magazine and he was smiling, unlike the severe look he had on his face in the picture frame.

She had a big smile on her face as she said to me, 'The first thing I want you to do is take that picture of Padre Pio out of the frame and put this one in instead. I don't like seeing unhappy faces.' She later said to me, 'It's so sad, whenever we see pictures of saints, that they always have sour faces. It's always better to have a smile on your face.' That's obviously what she wanted.

She loved that photograph and she loved him. He brought her much peace and great comfort. She would say, 'He's always looking out for me.' She was always positive. I never once went in to her when she was down, even though she had good reason to feel that way. She always had a smile on her face. Even when things would be bad, she'd say, 'It'll be alright. We'll be taken care of. I'll pray to Padre Pio and everything will be fine.'

I would meet other people and the first thing they might say was, 'Oh! I'm in a bad way. I can't do this and I can't do that.' Yet, even though Annie's ulcers might be very painful, especially the ones in her heels, she'd say, 'Don't worry. They'll be OK.' She never felt sorry for herself. If things went right, she'd say, 'That's thanks to himself on the mantelpiece.' In her own way, I think she was copying Padre Pio in her terrible struggle.

I know Annie's story isn't a miracle, but it's almost a miracle. Her love of Padre Pio enabled her to live a good life, despite all her problems. Maybe it tells us that he can help people through their lives and be at peace with themselves and everything that's happening around them. It can help them see the good in life. In my opinion, that's what happened in Annie's case anyway.

PAT, FROM COUNTY DONEGAL, explains the role of Padre Pio in his son's rehabilitation from a brain injury.

It all happened on 26 October 2003. That day, my son played Gaelic football for his team. He was 19 at the time. They won the football match and went for a few beers afterwards. The whole town was out as it was a big event. They had won the league and were promoted and it was a big celebration. I was there, too, giving my cousin a hand behind the bar. I wasn't joining in the festivities, but I was part of the whole thing.

My son's drink spilled over and he decided to go home and

get changed before they all went elsewhere. It was around ten o'clock at night. I said, 'I'll leave you home.' He said, 'No, no, stay where you are.' It was a good, clear night, not too dark or anything. So off he went, on his own, to home, which was just over a bridge and a turn to the left. It was only a five-minute walk away.

He walked over the bridge and he either stopped to make or receive a phone call. A car was coming and it hit him. He was only about two steps from safety when he was knocked down. He got a bad laceration on the back of his leg, but the main thing was head injuries. He either got them from the road or the car; either way, the head took most of the impact.

He was in a very bad way. His skull was fractured and he had swelling of the brain. He was unconscious. By the grace of God, the first man on the scene had knowledge of first aid and knew exactly what to do. He happened to be passing by in a car. He put my son in the recovery position and opened the airways and that played a big part in saving him.

I was still in the bar, but I heard that somebody had been killed at the bridge. I walked over, not realising what had taken place. I didn't hear it was my son until I was nearly there. Having been told that somebody had been killed, I feared the worst. But I then heard he was alive and that gave me hope.

By the time I got there, my son was wrapped in tinfoil and was being put into the back of an ambulance. It was clear that things were bad. There was blood coming from his nose and his ears and wherever. His head was badly swollen. He was rushed to the local hospital and we followed by car. Once they got there, he was brought into Intensive Care.

They immediately put him on a life-support machine and

started to work on him. They told us that things were bad. They said that the next hours were critical. First of all, it was the next four or five hours that were critical. Then it was the next 12 hours. After that, it was the next 24 hours. It was made clear to us that things were very serious and if there were any family members away, get them home.

My wife's mother was also there at the time and was very determined to get my son to the Royal Victoria Hospital in Belfast. Eventually, they sent two ambulances and a team down from the Royal and took him to Belfast. That was about a day or two after he had been knocked down. I remember him being taken away, wrapped in tinfoil and with tubes everywhere.

He was still in a deep coma when he got there. We were again told he was critical and very sick. His brain was still swelling badly. It wasn't coming down and it was getting worse if anything. They had to use drains. They were considering operating on him to remove a piece of the skull, which would let the brain swell freely. We were very worried about that.

I'm not sure who contacted Bill Mc Laughlin, the man who had the Padre Pio relic. My family always had great belief in the saint. My mother was very religious and had prayed to him down through the years. My wife's family also had faith in him. He was big in both of our families, so someone got in touch with Bill and he arrived about a week after the accident.

I have no idea how Bill got to see my son. Although we were always there, Bill got in and out without anyone seeing him. I still don't know how he did it to this day. We must have gone for tea or something. He phoned me afterwards to tell me he had been and gone. He said that he had brought in the mitten and had prayed. He also said, 'Your son will be grand. He'll be fine. Don't worry.'

LATER YEARS

Almost immediately, things improved. The swelling on my son's brain started to come down. His coma scale began to rise. The scale measures the level of coma a person is in. My son had been running at three, as deep into a coma as you can get. He started rising slowly. Initially, he didn't come up far, although he came up enough to be moved from Intensive Care to High Dependency.

We could see the first signs that things were improving. He opened up his eyes every now and again. He had finger movement. His body would start moving at certain times. We still didn't know what the outcome would be and we worried that my son might never properly recover. It was also being stressed that it would all take time. The good news, however, was that with the swelling coming down, the operation never took place.

After a fortnight in Belfast, where my son was cared for brilliantly, he was moved back to a hospital closer to home. He was still in a coma and it took four weeks, all told, for him to emerge from it. But he improved all the time. He started trying to talk and he began to write messages to us. Although he was paralysed down one side, we brought him up and down the corridor in an effort to improve that. My wife was with him every day and she put in a lot of time helping him to recover in so many ways.

We finally got him out for Christmas, after almost two months. They didn't want him to leave, but we insisted. We had set our sights on it, come what may. By that stage, he had lost three or four stone and was very weak. He could barely walk. But he was clearly improving and by January his recovery was good.

We had been told that his recovery would take 18 months,

at a minimum, in a rehabilitation centre and he would have to learn to walk and talk again. But it didn't happen like that. He never went back into hospital again and he is now absolutely grand. He is married, with a son. His mobility is fine and he can walk and talk. He is also back at work.

I attribute the big turning point – the bringing down of the swelling – to Padre Pio. That was critical. As regards the rest of it, my wife worked hard with him. She walked with him and did everything with him and basically rehabilitated him by herself. But if the swelling hadn't come down, they would have had to take the top of his skull off. If that had happened, he wouldn't be where he is today.

I also think the power of prayer had a massive role to play. So many people prayed for him, whether to Padre Pio or the Blessed Virgin or whoever. Our local community came out in force and they had Masses said and prayed. But I will always believe that the day Bill came in and the swelling stopped was the defining moment. It was my son's big turning point. It made all the difference. Something definitely happened and everything changed right after that.

MARY, FROM COUNTY DUBLIN, describes a visitation from Padre Pio around the time her husband was diagnosed with cancer.

In 2002, my husband wasn't looking well. He wasn't sick or complaining. He hadn't lost weight and he was eating and exercising. We used to go walking in the evening and he continued doing that. However, I felt he was a bit pale and had lost his sparkle. I felt that something wasn't right and I asked him to go to the doctor. He didn't feel there was any reason why he should, so he didn't go.

Later Years

At one stage, our children gave us a present of a weekend in a hotel in Galway. We went there and we were having our dinner on the very first evening. During the dinner, my husband developed very bad abdominal pain. He went to the loo and didn't appear back to the table for about 20 minutes. We had planned to go for a walk, but we didn't. Instead, we came back to Dublin early the following day, after breakfast.

He eventually went to the doctor and got a letter to go for a colonoscopy. There was a six-week wait. We were promised we would have the whole procedure done after Christmas. In the meantime, I was working nights, as I always did, and my husband would ring me at about two o'clock in the afternoon when he was about to come home from work. I would collect him. I used to do that, at this stage, because I didn't want him standing around waiting for a bus.

On 27 November, however, he rang me and said he was going to get a lift home and not to bother collecting him. I said, 'Fair enough. I will lie on in bed for another hour.' It was around two o'clock in the afternoon. I read the paper and rested. I said the Rosary, as I usually did, between three and four o'clock. Then, at around ten minutes to four, I decided to go downstairs for a drink and see if there was any post. I went downstairs, got a glass of milk and saw there was no post. I started to come back up again.

When I was at the end of the stairs, I got a beautiful, strong smell of flowers. It was like roses, lilies and violets. The smell got stronger and stronger as I came up the stairs. I had never experienced it before and I couldn't explain it. The only thing that entered my head was that my husband, who had hoovered the bedroom the day before, might have shaken some Shake n' Vac around. There had been a container of it in the house, which hadn't been used for years. That's all that came into my mind.

By the time I had opened the bedroom door, the smell was overwhelming. It was beautiful. I love flowers, yet I had never smelled anything like this before. I looked around and couldn't see anything different that might have caused it. I also thought, 'How come I didn't smell anything like that when I was going downstairs?' The next thing, the room became freezing cold. The temperature dropped. I got into bed and I covered myself up.

It was a cold, crisp day, with no clouds, and I lay there with the sun in my eyes. The light was shining in my face. It was extremely bright. Because of that, I turned over onto my left side, away from the sun. As I did so, I opened my eyes and got an awful fright. Padre Pio was beside the bed! I actually cursed and went down under the bedclothes. While I was there, I knew there was still a presence in the room. After a few minutes, I got a bit of courage and came back up again. Padre Pio was still there.

It was like he was kneeling down beside the bed. He wore a brown habit, with the hood over his head. He looked life-sized and his skin was ashen. Although pictures normally show him in pain, he seemed very happy. Because he was kneeling down, all I really could see was his face and hands, not his body. He had beautiful, smiling eyes and had a page in one hand. I wondered later about the page; maybe it was because he was delivering a message.

He looked at me and said, 'You have to pray harder.' At this stage, I was praying very hard because I guessed there was something wrong with my husband, although I never suspected anything like cancer. I thought maybe my husband had an ulcer. Padre Pio then said something I was never sure about afterwards. He either said he would be waiting to take me, or waiting to take my husband, to the Lord. I wasn't sure which. At the time, I thought it related to me and I was dying. I never linked it to my husband. I suppose I was in shock.

Padre Pio then became airborne and he moved away from my side of the bed. He moved over to my husband's side of the bed, made a sign of the cross on my husband's pillow and he disappeared through the door. There wasn't a sound throughout all of this. It took me a while to compose myself. I went out of the bedroom to see if he was still in the house. I had to sit on the stairs and my mouth was dry. I felt weak, although I wasn't sick and I was in good health. I went into the bathroom and drank some water. I really thought I would faint. I tried everywhere, upstairs and downstairs, but I saw nothing.

After he was gone, I realised that the visit by Padre Pio, and what he had said, related to my husband. I thought, 'He's come to bring me bad news.' When my husband came home, I told him what had happened, although I didn't say that I thought it related to him. He believed it. My children, who I told, believed it, too. I also knew I hadn't imagined it or dreamt it. My husband believed that, at some stage, the story should be told, but I didn't tell other people at the time, especially people at work.

Just after Christmastime, my husband was called in for his colonoscopy and he was told he had a tumour on his bowel. They were very good to him and took him in as soon as they had a bed. He had surgery and chemotherapy. The cancer then went from his bowel to his liver and he had surgery there. It then travelled to his lung and again to his liver. So it was very difficult for him and he didn't have an easy time; he got no break and he had no all-clear.

My husband did, however, survive for six years and he got more time than a patient with his complaints would normally get. They did everything for him in hospital, including clinical trials, and he didn't die until January 2009. He wanted to live and I think Padre Pio helped him to do that and he also helped me to cope. In particular, though, he helped my husband. I know that I wouldn't have had the courage that my husband had and I know many, many patients would have pulled out long beforehand.

What took place was very strange. I hadn't even been a devotee of Padre Pio. I wouldn't have prayed to him regularly. I would have prayed to Our Lady, the Lord, St. Thérèse and others, but not to him. I was, however, interested in him, especially the stigmata. I think, for some reason, he came to help us. So, after his first chemotherapy, my husband and I did travel to San Giovanni and I always prayed to Padre Pio afterwards. I also went back to San Giovanni in 2010.

I believe Padre Pio, as he promised, was there to meet my husband at the time that he died. I certainly know that my husband had a smile on his face as he passed away. He was in hospital at that stage. He was conscious, but he was bleeding and I could discern from the monitor that he had no blood pressure. They called me outside and said, 'He is dying.' I said, 'I know that.' So they decided not to resuscitate him, as he was going to go anyway. He was practically gone.

I was holding his hand as he slipped away. At the time, it was like he was looking into the distance and a calm smile came on his face. It was a smile I hadn't seen in a long time. He had a lovely, relaxed expression. He clearly saw somebody coming towards him; there was no doubt in my mind. It could have been any member of his family, but it could have been Padre Pio and I certainly hope it was. It was at that point that my husband took his last breath and he died.

JOHN, FROM COUNTY MEATH, believes that Padre Pio has been instrumental in his battle with cancer.

I first heard of Padre Pio through my grandmother. She would always be talking about him and praying to him. If there was thunder and lightning, she would pray to him. She also had pictures of him. She would tell me stories about his stigmata and how good he was. I was only about ten at the time and he had died just six years beforehand.

He caught my imagination right from the start. I felt there was something special about him. All you had to do was look at his face and you could see that. He had the look of a saint. You could also see love there. It almost felt that he was the reincarnation of Jesus, who had come back amongst us. So I was drawn to him from that time.

I was very religious at that stage and went to Mass every Sunday. I would pray every night. In bed, before I'd go to sleep, my brother would say, 'I know what you're doing, you're praying.' I might be saying a few Hail Marys and an Our Father. At that stage, however, Padre Pio didn't feature greatly, although I was aware of him and he was there in the background.

Later in life, when I was 37 years old, I was getting a lot of very bad headaches and I was constantly on painkillers. I was also getting strange sensations while I was in bed at night. I would be waking up and smacking my lips and getting pins and needles. I thought I was having nightmares.

One night, I got a terrible headache, which lasted for about four or five hours. I got physically sick and had to go up and lie on the bed and pull over the blinds and put my head under the pillow. I got a similar one on a different night. I woke up having bitten my tongue and there was froth coming out of my mouth and I was shaking. I had to go to the hospital as a result.

The hospital took MRI scans and CT scans and I was in there for about a week getting the tests done. Initially, they thought I had a stroke and they treated me for that. Unfortunately, things got worse and worse. I might be having six or seven or even up to ten of these seizures a day. Even with changes in the drugs I was on, nothing was working.

Throughout that time, people were giving me all sorts of relics, including relics of Padre Pio. I started praying to him in the morning and at lunchtime and at night. I would ask him to bless me and to intercede for me and to keep me healthy and strong. Yet there was no improvement in my condition and it was clear something serious was wrong.

Eventually, I was brought in for more tests and an MRI scan showed up that I had a tumour. It was a temporal lobe tumour, on the right-hand side. It was big, about the size of a medium-sized orange. They told me that it was inoperable in Ireland and they said to wait and see and they would observe how things went.

Fortunately, at the time, there was a girl back home from America and she had a magazine with her, which I read. There was this story in it about a Japanese surgeon who saved a girl's life. She hadn't been given long to live, but she was still alive some 15 or 20 years later. I decided to get in contact with him and he sent all my medical records on to another

Later Years

surgeon. They both looked at the records and they said they could operate.

When I travelled to America to have the operation in 2004, I brought some Padre Pio relics with me. I wanted to wear one of them during the operation and they let me put it inside one of my surgical stockings. I also asked my surgeon, who was Jewish, if he would wear one while he was operating. He did what I asked and put it in his pocket.

I knew, at the time, that Padre Pio would be with me. It made me feel so calm and at peace. I actually felt, if it didn't work and Padre Pio or Jesus didn't want me to live, then that was OK, too. I said to Padre Pio, 'If you don't want me to live, please take me to heaven and look after me.' As a result, I went into the operation with no fear whatsoever.

I had a four-hour operation and was in America for only about eight days, four of them in the hospital. They removed about 70 or 75 per cent of the tumour. They had to leave a little piece in there, about an inch in diameter. Afterwards, they said the operation was a great success and I would have only had three years to live if I hadn't had the tumour removed.

They also warned me, 'Cancer cells are like terrorists; you just don't know when they're going to pop back up again. But we have removed as much of your tumour as we could.' The good news is that, since then, there's been no regrowth of the tumour and I am, at present, some four years in remission. However, cancer can come back at any time, even after ten years, but I don't worry about that; I just keep going.

I now pray to Padre Pio every night and I feel he's looking after me. I've often gone to bed and cried while praying to him. Maybe that's because I'm so happy I have him. I feel it took many years for him to come to me, but I now know he's with me. I feel close to him and I believe there's an attachment there. I think he's around me all the time.

Recently, I had two dreams about him. I could actually see him in both. In one, I saw his face in front of me and in the other, about a week or two later, he was again standing facing me. It felt like he was letting me know he was there. It was like he was saying, 'I'm with you, John.'

Another night, I had a strange sensation in bed. I was lying on my left side and I could feel something touch me around my right shoulder and neck. I could actually feel a presence. I kept saying, 'Please don't go.' I eventually turned around and the first thing I saw was the photo of Padre Pio on the wall. It was a strange experience and it brought me a great feeling of peace.

I also went out to San Giovanni to thank him, along with Bill Mc Laughlin, who has a relic of Padre Pio. It was a very emotional visit. I met Fr. Ermelindo, who had looked after him and who was his secretary. He took out the cross Padre Pio used to use and he blessed me with it. I could feel Padre Pio there with me. I cried like I did on the day my daughter was born. It was the equivalent to my holding her in my arms.

I am definite it was Padre Pio who got me through the operation. It was he who pointed me in the right direction and brought me a miracle. He was always there for me and was looking after me. I don't think I'd be here now without him. It's hard to describe, but I think if you pray to him enough, and you ask for something, it will definitely happen.

Later Years

Catherine, from County Kerry, remembers how her son overcame horrific injuries incurred in a road accident. He was in his early 20s at the time it took place.

My son was in a bad hit-and-run accident in 2004. He was walking along the road with a group of his friends when a motorist ploughed into him. It was dark at the time. About six or seven of them were walking along. My son was last in line, but he was the one that got hit. He was thrown in the air and must have rolled off the car's bonnet and on to the road. He broke the windscreen of the car. It was absolutely terrible.

He was very badly injured. Both of his legs were dislocated at the knees, his left arm was broken and he had a huge gash in his liver, which caused an awful lot of blood loss. He had marks all over, but especially on his head. The legs and arms weren't the real problem, though; the major injury was to his brain and that was to prove the biggest concern. He was in a coma for about three weeks.

The ambulance came and he was then taken to the local hospital. He was assessed there and then moved to a bigger hospital, where he was put on life support. Throughout the first three weeks, there was no movement from him, nothing at all. By the middle of the second week, they had taken him out of an induced coma and were expecting him to come around. Unfortunately, there was no response. They checked his eyes every day, but there was nothing happening. The doctors were giving us the worst and nobody expected him to live.

We were all gathered there, devastated. We were in bits. He had been special to all of our family and the thought of him dying or not recognising us was awful. He was also dreadful to look at, as his body was twice its size from the bruising and swelling. Two sisters were so concerned that they stayed with him through every night. They would then go for a little rest and come back for the next night.

We were begging and imploring him to wake up. He was a big Elvis Presley fan and one of the sisters used to play Elvis into his ear. His friends also came and sat with him. The medical people wanted them to come and chat between themselves, to see if he would react. He might have reacted quicker to them than to us. But nothing happened. We just resigned ourselves and we actually spoke about what to do with his organs.

On the very first morning, before my son was transferred between hospitals, a local lady had sent us a very big, first-class relic of Padre Pio. It was a bit of white cloth in a big case. That stayed next to my son the whole time. We used to put it on his chest and leave it resting on him. Two people also came into the hospital with Padre Pio gloves. They would put the glove on his head and pray. I think Padre Pio went around with us during all that time.

We also went to Mass every day while he was in hospital and we had special Masses said as well. I prayed to lots of people, especially to those who had already gone, like my mother and father. But I also prayed to Padre Pio. I was very aware of him, although I didn't have relics or medals or anything like that. I would have heard of him from my mother, who remembered him from when he was still alive. I can recall her talking about him and she would always have his picture in her prayer book and would pray to him. She was a devotee.

Time went on and, one day, one of the girls saw my son's finger move. I think the medical people thought it was only an involuntary movement, but she wouldn't believe it. She felt something was going to happen and that gave us hope. His eyes then flickered one night and all hell broke loose. Whoever was sitting with him was very excited.

He eventually came out of the coma and we could see he was getting better and we knew that he was going to live. But we didn't know how much of a care he would be for us. We knew he would be severely damaged. For example, he wasn't able to move properly for a long time and his memory was affected. He was incontinent and refusing to eat. He couldn't use his hands for months.

Eventually, after eight weeks, he was transferred back to the local hospital and he then went into rehab. There was a long and difficult recovery ahead. Today, however, my son is very good. He had to have knee surgery, to reconstruct his knees, and his mobility came back. His memory also came back, although his short-term memory still wouldn't be great. He was back driving a car after about a year. While his whole life changed, he is working now and living a very normal life.

The doctors stated that my son's recovery was a miracle. About six years after the event, my daughter was at a wedding and she met one of the doctors who had looked after him. She hadn't seen him for years and was looking at him and trying to recognise him. She said to him, 'I think I know you.' He said, 'Well, I know you. Your brother was one of the few miracles I ever saw happen. He should never have lived.' He could remember everything about him and said he didn't think he would recover. 'I'll never forget you,' he said.

I believe what happened was a miracle. I would always say that. I also believe Padre Pio must have helped in my son's recovery. We were shocked that he recovered so well. We thought, at best, that he would be brain-damaged and we would have to look after him for the rest of his life. But that didn't happen. I believe the prayers worked and, although we prayed to a lot of people, we could put Padre Pio on the top of the list.

Padre Pio also stays with us. He seems to have a habit of just popping up out of nowhere. We find this quite eerie. My husband says the same thing. He carries him in his pocket all the time and I do it, too. It might be a picture or a medal or a leaflet with a little relic.

I have often put my hand in the pocket of a coat I haven't worn for a while, or opened an old handbag, and Padre Pio is there, as if he is reminding us. I was visiting someone lately, who was sick, and I opened my wallet and found a beautiful laminated card. I was able to give it to her. He just comes from nowhere.

We also go to a Padre Pio prayer group as a sort of thanksgiving. I have been over to San Giovanni a few times as well. My daughters went there, too. We go because we think there is something very special about him. Sometimes, when I look at his statue, I think he is giving me a cross look. But, whenever I go to his prayer meetings, I always come away feeling better. And, after what happened with my son, I know he is a healer. I have no doubt about that.

ANN, WHO COMES ORIGINALLY FROM COUNTY ROSCOMMON but who now lives in County Offaly, recovered from ear problems after being blessed with a Padre Pio relic. It happened in 2005.

My devotion to St. Padre Pio goes back about 30 years. I stumbled on him at the time. I grew up in a very religious family who said the Rosary and went to Mass and travelled to Knock, but I never knew about Padre Pio. I had relics of St.

Thérèse and things like that, but Padre Pio never surfaced in my life.

I can't remember how I was introduced to him, yet when I came across him I seemed to develop an instant attachment. There was a definite connection there. He took me over. He was a very holy man who suffered a lot. He also was a man of my time; he was alive when I was. I thought, 'I love this man.' I felt, 'This is the person who can help me. He can do more for me than anybody else.'

I soon started to pray to him a lot. If I was running short of time, I would neglect other prayers, but not the prayer to him. I wouldn't go anywhere without having his relic in my bag. Whenever the glove would appear, I would go through fire and water to get to it.

I even brought him to hospital with me. A few years ago, I was about to undergo an operation and I am claustrophobic. I had to have a scan, but I was terrified about going into the scanning machine. The only way I would go for the scan was with my eyes closed and a vision of Padre Pio's face in front of me, in my mind. He accompanied me everywhere in my life.

I had some awful earaches for many years. I had one ear infection after the other. The pain was wicked, up the side of my head. One day, I felt there was no power in my jaw. Even in the middle of summer, I would be out with a scarf or a hat on me. The man in the shop nearby used to call me 'Peig Sayers' because of the scarf I'd wear! I was worried I had cancer or a brain haemorrhage or something like that. I also wondered if I was going to go deaf.

I went to hospitals and they tested me and did scans and they said I had hearing loss. They concluded it was caused by sinus. I was on huge amounts of antibiotics, but things didn't improve. My sleeping was becoming badly affected. I would always wake up with the pain. I would lie on one side to keep the ear covered, but when I would turn over to the other side the pain would wake me up. It was unbelievable.

When the statue of Padre Pio was being unveiled and being blessed outside the church here in Banagher, County Offaly, in 2005, I was there in the middle of it. That was a big moment for all of us. I remember it was a windy day and the weather wasn't great, but I felt, 'We really have him here with us now.'

Someone from Cork was there with a relic of Padre Pio. A person pointed him out to me. I got into the queue, waiting to be blessed. I focused on my ears as I walked up the queue. I don't even know what relic he had, because I didn't look up. I didn't talk to him; I just focused. I really believed it could help me and I felt very happy and privileged to be there.

Almost immediately afterwards, I had no pain in the ears and I had no infections. I realised that the pain was gone and I was going out without a hat or a scarf. Now, when it's windy, I can go out without wearing any protection on my head. I also don't need any antibiotics or to run to the doctor. I can sleep with no pain. The problem has never come back and it can be all traced to that day the statue was blessed in Banagher.

Since then, the Padre Pio glove has meant a lot to me. I have been blessed with one of the gloves probably nine or ten times. When it arrives to a place near me, I'll be there. I also go up to the statue in Banagher a lot. I get out of the car and pray to it. If it is at night and dark, I might sit in the car and roll down the window and talk to him and pray to him.

I think he was a really wonderful man. He's touched so many people and he has helped so many as well. When I now hear of anyone who is unwell, I always suggest getting the glove or a relic. If I ever have a problem, I go to him straight away. I believe he's always with me and he makes the impossible possible. With his help and his power, you can do anything, even move mountains.

TRACY, FROM DUBLIN but who lives in County Mayo, tells how Padre Pio ensured that she arrived on time for a rendezvous at Knock Airport.

Back in 2005, I worked as a tour rep in Lourdes and I loved it. I would meet people as they arrived on their flights, welcome them, put them on the bus and give them a quick overview about Lourdes on the way in. I'd meet them every day, in their hotels, for the five days they were there and tell them what the daily programme was. I would accompany them on all the different things they used to do. I got to know Lourdes from back to front.

I did it for one season and then left for Medjugorje, where I did some voluntary work. I thought I was going there for just a week, so I only took hand-luggage. I left my two bigger bags in Lourdes, in one of the hotels, containing most of my clothes and my personal belongings. The plan was that, after Medjugorje, I would come back to Lourdes, collect my bags and then head home to Ireland.

I ended up staying in Medjugorje for a couple of months. I had been there before, in 2000, and it had transformed my life completely. It opened up my eyes and did a lot for my faith. I went back to all the sacraments and all the beliefs I had as a child. It woke up what was already in me. After this latest visit, however, I travelled straight back to Dublin from Medjugorje, leaving my bags in Lourdes.

About a year-and-a-half or two years later, the bags were

still in Lourdes. I eventually realised that a group from Knock were going there on their annual pilgrimage. I asked if they could pick up the bags and they agreed. The plan was that, when their flight was landing back at Knock, I would go to the airport and pick the bags up from there.

I had arranged with a friend that he would give me a lift to the airport. I don't know where my own car was at the time, maybe in the garage or somewhere else like that. Unfortunately, my friend completely forgot about the arrangement. It went out of his mind completely and he wasn't arriving back.

Time was passing by and the flight was about to land and I was panicking. I was wondering, 'What am I going to do? I really wanted to be there when the flight was landing because the Knock pilgrimage were doing me a favour and I didn't want them to be arriving at the airport and me not being there. I wanted to make it as easy on them as possible.

I kept phoning him, trying to get him to come back, but I couldn't get him as his phone was off. I didn't know where he was. I then just said to my guardian angel, 'Will you please go to St. Pio and ask him to go to his guardian angel and his guardian angel can tell my friend that he has to come back.' I suppose I hoped that Padre Pio's guardian angel would kind of tap my friend on the shoulder and remind him!

It was something that I remembered about Padre Pio from before. He had talked about 'sending guardian angels' if you needed something. It wasn't surprising that I turned to him as I always loved him along with Our Lady. I know my mother once had a lump in her breast and it disappeared after she was blessed with a glove of St. Pio. That was probably the first I heard of him. My mother's friend used to talk about him a lot as well. She had great faith in him.

Later Years

I had also gone to San Giovanni around 2004, before Lourdes. I went everywhere there, including to the chapel and the tomb. I signed up to be one of his spiritual children. I was really very impressed by the way he heard confessions and the way he could see right through people. It highlighted how important it is to be absolutely sincere in your confession because you're not fooling anyone but yourself. I was also struck by his sanctity.

Anyway, regarding my bags, I thought, 'I'm desperate. I will have to attempt this,' so I asked my guardian angel to help. Not long afterwards, my friend arrived back. I was saying to him, 'I was trying to ring you,' but I think his phone was still off. I told him about the arrangement again and he said, 'I forgot about it completely.' I then said, 'Come on, quick, we have to go right now.'

When I was on the way to the airport, I was explaining to my friend what I did to get him to come back. He replied, 'I was just sitting in the car, reading a newspaper, in the sun, relaxing. My phone was off.' Apparently, he had gone off up some country lane just to read in the sun in the car. He was taking a bit of time off.

He then said, 'It's really weird because, when I was there, I could suddenly feel this thing coming over me, telling me I had to get back.' It was like someone was tapping him on his shoulder. He said he didn't know what it was about, but he knew he had to get into the car, start the engine and get back to the house. He didn't even know why he had to do it; he didn't remember he had to collect the bags. The message, he said, was very clear: he just had to get back.

I wasn't surprised; just excited. I was delighted that going through Padre Pio had worked. That was the first time I had tried it. It was definitely the first time I had tried it and got confirmation from the other person that it had worked. It was clear proof to me of what Padre Pio could do.

Since then, Padre Pio has become part of my life. He always seems to pop up and make himself known to me. He had to struggle with things, like the stigmata and the spiritual warfare he went through with the Devil. He had to go through it all and he understands. So if I'm struggling now, I call on him. No matter who is struggling, they should do the same.

I also still ask my guardian angel to go to him. It might be to contact somebody or to tell them something. I take it for granted so much that I don't even notice I'm doing it. I believe that was the way that my friend received the message and felt a need to come back, so I have no doubt it works.

ANGELA, FROM COUNTY CARLOW, talks about her husband's triumph over a brain tumour.

In 2006, my husband Jim started coming home from work complaining that he had taken a turn. He said he would just go blank. It would happen about once a week and he was worried. I didn't take a whole lot of notice, partly because I hadn't seen them and partly because he looked perfect when he'd come in at night. He was hard-working and he loved his few drinks at the weekend, so I put the turns down to that.

In August of that year, a whole gang of us from my family went to Spain on holiday. I come from a big family and 14 of us went. It was meant to be a big, happy occasion. We never had the chance to go before and it was a lovely idea. Unfortunately, we were only there for perhaps a day or so before my husband had another one of his turns.

I remember he was on the sofa and he started staring into space. I was talking to him and there was no reaction, not even a movement of the head. He turned grey-green and was pumping sweat. When he came out of it, he pointed up at the ceiling and said, 'Angela, there's a cup of tea up there for you.' It lasted about four or five minutes and was very strange.

I was terribly worried, especially because we were in Spain. I asked myself, 'What can we do?' We talked about getting home, but the cost would have been huge. Anyway, once the turn was over, he seemed to be back to himself. I thought we would just keep an eye on things and stick it out for the two weeks.

He had a couple of turns following that. One morning, he disappeared and I went looking for him. I found him fallen down in the street as if he was drunk. He had fallen so hard that he had split himself open and was badly cut. It was a nightmare to see. After that, he was fine again. Even though we were having a rotten holiday, we felt there was nothing we could do but stick it out.

When we got back to Ireland, we went to a doctor who thought it was epileptic fits. Jim was then referred to a hospital for tests. Eventually, a scan was done and they discovered that he had a massive tumour. It was in the left frontal lobe and it was the cause of what was happening to him. Jim's reaction was brilliant. He felt, 'It is what it is,' but I fell asunder and couldn't cope.

We were told that he would need an operation and that the prospects were poor. They said there was a 70 per cent chance that he wouldn't make surgery. They also said that, even if he did make it, he'd be either brain-damaged or paralysed down one side. I will never forget the Friday that we were told. I suppose legally they have to tell you, but it was hard to hear it; it was all so blunt.

He had the operation on the Monday. They brought him down to theatre at about 11 o'clock and he didn't return until 8.30. It was the longest day of my life. I must have done 600 rounds of the hospital. They eventually brought him back and I spoke to him very briefly. I could see that he could move and wasn't paralysed. We were both delighted with that.

They told us that the operation had gone as well as they expected, but they wouldn't know anything for a few days. They also told us that the tumour was stage 4, which is the worst you can get. Because of where the cancer was, they had taken most of it away, but they couldn't get rid of it all. They couldn't get right into the stem. They also said that he would need chemotherapy and radiotherapy, but that wouldn't happen until after Christmas.

They warned us that, even with the chemotherapy and the radiotherapy, there still wasn't very much hope. They also mentioned that he would need another big scan at the end of November. I knew immediately this would be the last chance we'd have. They then let him home on Halloween night, which I remember because they were letting off bangers in the street.

One day, shortly afterwards, I was in my car and I heard on the radio that a Padre Pio mitten was coming to Carlow. I remember turning up the radio to listen to what they were saying. That evening, I rang the radio station and asked for the phone number of the man involved. It turned out to be Brendan Byrne, from Tullow, and they got me his phone number. I spoke to him and he invited us over to his house so that my husband could be blessed with the mitten, which is what we did.

At one stage, when we were there, I remember looking at my husband and I thought he was taking another turn. His face looked very strange. Later, on the way home, I asked him,

Later Years

'Why were you making a face in the house?' He said, 'I got a strong smell.' I asked him, 'What was the smell like?' He said, 'I don't know, it was strange.' Straight away, I said, 'That was Padre Pio!'

For days afterwards, both upstairs and downstairs at home, he kept getting that smell. He got it everywhere that he went. I wondered what it was. As it happened, Brendan Byrne had given me a gift of a Rosary beads. It was sealed in a plastic packet in a little white box. I had put it in my underwear drawer and had never opened it. When I opened the plastic, it released a smell of flowers and, when I gave the beads to my husband, he said, 'Yes, that's the smell I was getting.'

They were obviously scented Rosary beads, but you couldn't get any smell off them until they were opened. It couldn't have been that the smell he got earlier was from them because the bag they were in had been sealed. They were in a box as well. They were also in the back of my underwear drawer and he was getting the smell even in the kitchen or all over the house. I, too, got the smell off the beads, although I had never got it before.

I thought a lot about what was happening. I felt that it had something to do with Padre Pio, but I didn't know what it meant. Was Padre Pio coming to collect Jim? Or was Jim getting better? I just didn't know.

Jim eventually had the scan and we went back up to the hospital at the start of December for the results. I had a Padre Pio medal in my hand. I held it so tight that my nails crushed right into my palm. I remember there was a huge trolley in the clinic, that day, containing everyone's scans. Unfortunately, the secretary couldn't find my husband's scan on the trolley. Suddenly, I spotted this huge yellow envelope flying out of the trolley and across the floor. It was my husband's scan! It was all so strange.

We went in to the doctor and he put all the scans up on the wall. He pointed at the first one and the second one and the latest one and he said, 'Whatever you're doing, keep on doing it.' He had this big L-shaped desk and he pushed it out of the way so we could come closer and look at the latest scan. He said, 'There's the last one. The cancer is gone!' There was nothing there. We were shocked. My husband said, 'What do you mean, it's gone?' It was simple: there was nothing there. Everything was gone.

We went to San Giovanni the following August. We brought home with us a three-foot statue of Padre Pio. We didn't even get charged for the weight of it on the flight. It's now in the kitchen. When I'm in the kitchen and worried about something, I go over and put my hand on his hand and everything is OK.

Ever since then, everything's been perfect. Seven years later, there's no trace of the cancer. I attribute everything to Padre Pio. He always answered our prayers. I believe, 100 per cent, that he's the man who did it and, if only for that, I love him to death. I remember saying to a woman, one day, 'If he was alive today, I'd marry him!' She was very religious and wasn't impressed. She said, 'He wasn't the marrying type.' But I love him that much, I would!

MIKE, FROM COUNTY CORK, recalls how Padre Pio helped his young son cope with spina bifida.

My son was born in 2006, having been diagnosed with spina bifida prior to birth. He was a very sick baby. The birth was rough and the delivery went on for a long time. Although he was eventually born successfully, he needed to have emergency surgery within ten days. The surgery was done to reduce fluid on the brain. He had a further three operations in the first four months.

It was a very tough time. We might get three or four days with him at home and he would be back into hospital. All we were doing was going from home to hospital or hospital to home. I remember he was once getting caught for breath and we had to rush him in. He found it difficult to breathe and it scared the wits out of us. It was all very tense.

Despite all that was happening, he was a wonderful child. Most sick children don't move and you would know they are sick. But he had a smile for everyone, despite being in hospital for so long. His attitude was wonderful. He was great on that score. All the doctors and nurses were excellent, too, and I could never say a word against them.

At one stage, when my son was about six months old, they were looking to do another operation where they would take off the back of the skull and relieve the pressure. It was a big operation. At ten o'clock in the morning, the operation was going ahead. However, by about two o'clock, we were told that it wasn't being done.

They felt it wouldn't do any good and there would be no difference in the outcome whether we did the operation or not. The impression we were left with was that there was nothing for us but palliative care. We wondered, 'What's going on here?' The operation wasn't done and, in hindsight, I believe it would have done more damage than good.

That morning, I had been searching for a priest to christen my son. One priest didn't want to do it. He said, 'It doesn't matter if you don't get him christened because your intention is to do it.' I didn't go along with that. I met another priest and he said, 'No problem at all.' He was christened in the hospital at about 7.30 that evening.

About ten minutes or 20 minutes later, this man from Cork came in to bless our child. He was a friend of my dad's. My father had said, 'I have a friend who is into Padre Pio and he has some relics. He could come in and give a blessing.' I didn't know the man from Adam. I had said, 'Grand, grand, not a bother.'

I actually didn't see the blessing. There were lots of people inside in the room, including my mam and dad. Because we all couldn't fit inside, I was standing outside the door. All I could see was this fellow inside doing his thing and blessing my son. I felt, at that stage, 'Things are going to change' and I felt a huge difference after it. I felt a light shining over us and I thought that things were going to be OK. There definitely was something happening with the child after the visit.

Within four or five days, my son came home with us from hospital and the big thing afterwards was that he wasn't sick. Since then, if he was in a hospital even for an hour up to last September – when he had to have another operation as a seven-year-old – that would have been it. The child had been in hospital every week up to that. He's certainly not in palliative care and, if you now saw this kid, you would think there was no way he could ever have been.

Although he's been in a wheelchair since he was 12 months old, he's into cycling and swimming, he's doing karate and tag rugby, absolutely everything. He's one of these children that, no matter what happens, he is able to fight his corner. He is no hassle and would never say anything to offend you or hurt you. He is a very good kid.

He can converse with anyone. On one occasion, when he was

about three years of age, he met with Brian Crowley, the MEP. A few of us were chatting away to Brian and my son came up and was looking at him. It was probably the first time he saw an adult in a wheelchair. He was saying, 'Look at my wheelchair. Where is your spoke guard?' He had no bother and was chatting to Brian like he knew him for the last 20 years. It was great to see.

I'm not a religious person, but something definitely happened that evening. I felt things were going to be OK and that the child, while he was never going to be running around, was going to be fine. The difference between the child we had and the child we now have is remarkable; they are two ends of the spectrum.

As far as I'm concerned, Padre Pio is the man. I think we were in big trouble at the time. My dad had fierce faith in him and he believed that Padre Pio would help us and that he did help us. I think he helped us when we needed him. I know it happened because I was there. And, while I pray to a lot of people, Padre Pio would certainly be in my top three.

LIZ, WHO COMES FROM COUNTY DONEGAL but who lives in the UK, describes the miraculous revival of her boyfriend Jason from a dreadful sporting accident.

Jason and I met in Australia in 2006, at the Opera House in Sydney. We just happened to bump into each other. I was on a world trip and he was about to go back to New Zealand, where he was teaching at the time. I eventually went to New Zealand, which I had planned to do anyway. We met there again and we fell madly in love. We just knew we were right for each other. Everything was so romantic and lovely. It was like something out of heaven. I was so excited.

Eventually, Jason made his way back to England, where he was from. I was back working in Ireland by then. I would travel over at weekends and we would spend time together. At that stage, Jason was into all sorts of sports, including sailing, surfing and skiing. He was brilliant at them all. But he then decided to take up kite surfing because there wasn't really any opportunity for the other sports in Morecambe, where he was living.

One weekend, I was over with him and he dropped me off at the airport for my return trip to Ireland. We had just got engaged about a week before that and I was pregnant at the time. He left me at the airport at about three o'clock and dashed off to meet a friend at the beach, where he planned to do some kite surfing. There was actually a gale that day and he thought, 'Maybe I shouldn't go up.' But he decided to go ahead with it.

While he was still standing down on the beach, the kite lifted him about 20 or 30 feet up off the ground. The wind suddenly dropped and he fell on his head. He landed on the hard sand. Blood came pumping out of his nose. He had a skull fracture, which caused the bleeding. He was also unconscious. The friend who was with him is a doctor and, when he saw him, he thought there wasn't much hope.

The air ambulance came and took Jason to hospital. He was in a very bad way. He was just next to brain-dead. His pupils were dilated and weren't responding to light, which didn't look good. At that stage, I had arrived back in Ireland. They rang me up and I knew immediately that there was something wrong. I was told what happened and that it looked bad. I was basically told that Jason wouldn't survive. I was absolutely devastated.

Within an hour or two, they took Jason into surgery. He was on the operating table for seven hours. I eventually got a phone call from the surgeon to say that his blood wouldn't clot. He asked me was Jason on medication which might be causing that to happen. But he wasn't. He was pumping blood and he had to have eight pints transfused that night. It was looking bad because of that, too.

I flew over as quickly as I could. When I got to the hospital, Jason was covered in tubes. He was on a respirator, with his mouth wide open and this huge tube going down his throat. He was hooked up to all these machines. One machine was checking on the pressure in his brain. He was also in a coma and was heavily sedated. It was quite shocking to see.

He survived the first night, which was a great relief. Every single day, from then on, there was a huge sense of crisis. I can remember the surgeon told us that it didn't look like he was going to survive. They couldn't control the pressure on his brain because it was so high. They said, 'We may have to take out a piece of skull to relieve the pressure and, if that doesn't work, we may have to take out bits of brain.' I was freaked by that.

I begged God to let him live. I said, 'Even if he spends the rest of his life in a vegetative state, I just want to be there for him. Jesus, that's all I ask.' My friend sent over some medals and a Padre Pio relic from Ireland that her father had. My dad then brought over a relic of Padre Pio that we found through the book *Padre Pio: The Irish Connection*. I think that it was a little casket and it stayed right beside his bed. Another relic was arranged for us through a person in Ireland. So we had relics with him all the time.

I felt at that time that the only hope I had was that Jason

would be cured by a miracle. I prayed to Padre Pio every night on my knees that it would happen. I took a full hour on my knees, crying and praying and crying again. I begged Padre Pio and I begged Jesus to let him survive. I did a novena as well. I didn't know what I was going to do if he died. The hope I got through prayer is what kept me alive. I really felt that Padre Pio was going to bring him back. It was the only thing I had to cling to. Without that, and the constant loving support and prayers of our family and friends, I couldn't have continued.

Jason really turned around after that. Things started settling down and there was a sense that he wasn't going to die. He eventually started to wake up. One night, while I was sitting there, I noticed that Jason was kind of frowning. It was the first sign of consciousness. I went, 'Oh, my God!' Soon after, he lifted his arm up in the air and started trying to open one of his eyes. I also had to have a scan, at that time, because of the baby. When I told Jason it was going to be a baby boy, he squeezed my hand. It was a massive sense of relief for us that he was conscious.

After that, he recovered surprisingly well. He was soon able to give a 'thumbs up' to the doctor in answer to a question. He also started communicating. He could write things down. It was lovely that he came back so well, although it really was a hugely slow process that followed. He still had to have nine operations within his first year. He also had many setbacks and developed lots of infections. When he left hospital, he was in a wheelchair. And, though he's fine now, he's still coming back to his full self all these years later.

I believe that what happened was nothing short of miraculous. Jason is now fully physically recovered, which they once said wouldn't happen. He can walk and can go skiing now, despite the fact that the people in the hospital had told us, 'He will not stand or walk again.' He has gone surfing and sailing. He has gone to the gym. He cooks every night. But the big thing he has not gone back to is kite surfing. He is banned from that!

I think Padre Pio saved Jason's life. I felt at the time that it was because of him that he came out of the coma. I think it was he who brought about Jason's recovery. We prayed and prayed to him and I feel that we have been blessed. He has blessed every single aspect of our lives. Our son was born and he's wonderful. We got married in Donegal in 2009, which was brilliant. We went on honeymoon. And, most importantly, Jason is alive and has come back so well. I put that down to Padre Pio.

VERONICA, FROM COUNTY KERRY, describes the saint's role in her son's recuperation following a near-fatal car crash.

My son was in a car accident back in 2007. Somebody was overtaking him and seemingly skidded on ice. He just touched my son's car and it went spinning. He lost control and ended up hitting a pier in a wall. The accident was near-fatal. Every part of the car was bashed in, except for the little cocoon in the front seat where he was sitting.

Somebody phoned for the fire brigade and the ambulance. They arrived along with the Guards. By that stage, my son's heart had stopped beating. He was totally unconscious and they could find no pulse, so they presumed he was dead. They still were extremely careful and took him out of the car. He was then taken off to hospital.

At the hospital, they found out that he had swelling of the brain. His lungs were badly damaged and he was hypoxic. They thought they'd have to remove his left lung, it was so bad; the right lung wasn't much better. Loads of vertebrae were broken. They really had no hope, although they put him on a life-support machine.

We were devastated and we rushed to the hospital. When we got there, he looked perfect and I spoke to him as I spoke to him every day. The nurses must have thought I was mad. He couldn't respond. Normally, they would have moved him straight up to Dublin, but his vital C2 and C7 vertebrae were damaged and they couldn't risk moving him.

For five full days, we had to wait. It was terrible just sitting there. I am a Minister of the Eucharist and I was supposed to give out communion the day after the accident had happened. I said to my husband, 'There's nothing we can do here, so why don't we go to Mass and I can give out communion?' I felt I had to do something.

As it happened, it was a healing Mass and I'll never forget it. I prayed to everyone, including Padre Pio. My father, when he was dying, had great faith in him. There was a picture of Padre Pio in his room. I will never forget, after one very bad night, he said to my mother, while pointing at the picture, 'He looked after me last night.' So I prayed and prayed at the Mass and we got great healing out of it.

I knew a lot about Padre Pio at the time. I remember, when I was at secondary school, I went to a talk about Padre Pio. We were told about his stigmata and where he had lived and everything else. I thought his life story was wonderful. He was a most unusual, strange man. He was exceptional and out on his own, so private and so good to other people. He was also absolutely straight with everyone and that appealed to me.

Later Years

Not long after the Mass, probably on the same day, a man from Cork was arriving in the hospital with a relic of Padre Pio. A girl that I knew, who was working in the hospital, sent him up to my son. When I saw the relic, I couldn't believe it. I couldn't believe I had this sacred thing in my hand. It was divine.

We put the relic up to my son's lungs. The man prayed with us. It all went on for about 15 or 20 minutes and it made me feel great. I couldn't believe what had happened and that such a precious relic had arrived. I told all the family and they were delighted, especially my mother.

Two days afterwards, my husband's sister-in-law arrived with another Padre Pio relic. I got her into Intensive Care, which was a difficult thing to do as they didn't want people going in. I think she said the same prayers. Afterwards, when we were back out in the waiting-room, she said, 'Put that by your left lung, inside your coat.' I did and I never got as much peace as I got that night. I got great comfort from it.

The next day, they put on what's called a halo. They drill holes in the patient's skull and put a cage into the head with spikes coming out of it. It's used to keep the head still. Getting it on was big progress. They also found out, that day, that my son's spinal cord wasn't broken, which was great news. They hadn't been able to do anything up to that because they were afraid that even if they moved him a tiny bit he'd be gone.

There was a long road of recovery ahead after that, but we were into a different phase. Although he got loads of infections and things like that, we now knew he was going to live. While he didn't wake up for quite a long time afterwards, and I knew things wouldn't be fully right, we were able to draw our breath for a change.

The recovery itself was brutal. It was intensive and affected the whole family. He became agitated and didn't always know what he was doing. He had lost a lot of weight. I massaged his legs every day, so that it would help him walk again. I was dreading how hard it would be for him to put one foot in front of the other. Eventually, however, the time came when he actually put one foot in front of the other and it was great to see that.

It was also great to hear him speak again. Initially, he was only able to mumble. One day, the speech therapist got out of him my name and my husband's name and his name and his address. I couldn't believe it when I heard it. It's amazing what they can do. Another day, I opened one of the cards that had arrived and asked him, 'What does it say?' He mumbled out, 'Get well soon.' I thought, 'My God!' That was a very big moment.

In all, my son was in hospital for over three-and-a-half months. He is now well and able to walk and talk again. He was supposed to be gone. He was even gone by the time he was brought into the hospital. But, today, he is still very much alive.

I don't know if we were deserving of Padre Pio's healing. Perhaps he was healed because he was always a very good person, looking after both his grandmothers, who were mad about him. He was very good with lots of other people, too; afterwards, people told me how he would stop on the road and change a tyre for them. He never looked for praise, so I think he deserved help.

The good Lord, the angels and Padre Pio must have been looking down on him. And I know that we were brought a miracle. My son believes that, too. My prayers, not only to

Padre Pio but to the Divine Mercy, were answered. And, for the rest of my days, I will never forget Padre Pio, who came to us in our darkest hour.

MARIE, FROM COUNTY KERRY, recalls Padre Pio's role in her young daughter's battle with a tumour.

My daughter developed a pain in her stomach back in 2007. It seemed to be a straightforward pain, but she had it for a couple of days. I said I would take her along to the doctor. I thought it was a very simple visit for a problem which would be easily resolved. We went to the doctor and ten minutes later we were off to the local hospital. Within a couple of hours, we were going to Dublin.

They did scans and tests in Dublin and we were there for a couple of days. It turned out to be a kidney tumour. It was all so shocking and unreal. She was only eight years old at the time. Our lives were turned upside down. Everything seemed to be crumbling. I was devastated and so was my family; we are very close. I don't know where I got the strength. I think I just went into some kind of shock.

They told me that the scans showed it had spread to her lungs. I never said anything about how serious it was to my daughter; instead, I just told her she had to have an operation. I told her she had a tumour, but a tumour to an eight-year-old means nothing; they wouldn't know what it is. We then came home to Kerry.

Around that time, I saw a story in a paper about a couple who were praying to St. Padre Pio. I tracked them down and they told me about this man in Cork who had relics. He was the nicest man you could meet and had great devotion. We talked to him and he was so calming. He spoke about angels and Padre Pio. He prayed over my daughter. I immediately said, 'This is it! She is going to get better!'

I also got this little Padre Pio relic from a neighbour, which I brought everywhere with me. It's a little picture of the saint, with a piece of a relic on the back of it. It was always in my pocket and I took it everywhere. I got so many other relics and prayers and cards from other people. I started saying a novena to him every day. Although I had heard of him before, I hadn't any devotion to him. It wasn't until then that I turned to him and Our Lady.

I would talk to him all the time. I would always ask that my daughter could have a normal, healthy, happy life. That's all I ever wanted and that's what I prayed for. I asked for that at the time and I have asked for that every day since. I also asked that he would take this thing, this tumour, out of our lives. Most importantly, I prayed and prayed and prayed.

We were told that the operation would take about two hours, but it took between four-and-a-half and five hours. It went very well and they removed everything. I was so naïve that I thought, 'That's it. We can now go home and get back to normal.' I didn't realise that there was chemotherapy and radiotherapy to follow.

Around that time of the operation in Dublin, she got the Gooch's boots. Kerry had won the All-Ireland and some of the team came into the hospital with the cup. Colm Cooper was with them and he gave the Kerry girl his boots. They are blue and white and we keep them in a glass case. She was thrilled to get them. He was really nice; a quiet young fellow. It was a good start, just lovely.

She went back up for the chemotherapy and radiotherapy. It took its toll and wore her out. She felt very sick. She got

LATER YEARS

weaker and weaker and lost a lot of weight. Her weight fell to about three-and-a-half stone. She became a bag of bones. She also became very tired and very jaded. It was an unbelievably rough time and she was in a bad way.

I think I spent the whole time, that year, just praying. I would sit at her feet and pray. I would do it all day. I prayed up in Dublin, in the hospital. I did it everywhere, not just to Padre Pio but to Our Lady and St. Thérèse. I probably prayed to everyone, but Padre Pio was my main one. I promised him that when everything was over I would go to San Giovanni to say, 'Thank you,' which I did.

One day, during that year, while I was going up in the car to Dublin, I got a smell of flowers. It was a beautiful smell of fresh flowers. My mum and dad were with me. I asked my mum if she could smell it, too, and she couldn't. My dad couldn't smell it either. It definitely wasn't coming from any gardens or anything like that. It lasted for about two minutes. I said, 'St. Pio is here. Everything is going to be fine.'

After it was all over, my daughter got stronger and stronger. She put on weight. She got life back into her. It was a joy to see it happen. On 1 May, we got results showing that everything was clear. She just had to finish off the treatment and after that we never looked back.

She is now absolutely perfect, on top of the world. She is back at school and can do everything. She plays basketball and goes out with her friends to discos at the youth club. She is just like any happy-go-lucky teenager. I often look at her and cry with joy. I recently saw her in her first school play. I said, 'Please, God, don't let me cry!' I was so proud. We never look back; we just go onwards and upwards. And we don't mention that nasty, horrible word – tumour.

I put my daughter's recovery mainly down to Padre Pio and also to Our Lady. He always loved Our Lady, so I put them side by side. I think Padre Pio kept me sane and kept me together and I think he played a big part in healing my daughter. I prayed and prayed to him all the time and he heard me. I often say to people, 'I prayed her better.'

I still say a novena to Padre Pio every day and I still have my precious picture relic, which is now in tatters. That little relic is under my pillow at the moment. I also have a statue of him on my window, along with pictures. I believe he is a great intercessor, a kind man and was kind to me and my daughter. Padre Pio is my man!

MARY, FROM COUNTY OFFALY, recovered from her depression in 2008 after discovering Padre Pio.

I started to suffer from depression in 2008. It hit me badly. I'd get headaches and feel very black and horrendously dark. My sleep was affected and my energy levels fell. I lost interest in life and I'd get strange feelings and ugly thoughts. Basically, there were suicidal thoughts involved. I didn't know what was happening and I kept quiet about it for a while. It was a scary time.

I eventually went off to the doctor to get something for it. I was prescribed antidepressants. I thought that they would be the answer. Unfortunately, I had a bad reaction to the medication and that intensified things a hundredfold. The first night I took the medication, I was shaking and had palpitations and couldn't sleep. I had an awful time just trying to keep myself together.

I rang my doctor, who was surprised by what had happened and suggested that I might try something to relax. After the reaction I had from the antidepressants, I said, 'It's alright. I'll just try and get through it.' I was afraid to try another medication and I decided I wasn't going to take any more prescription drugs. So I went it alone and decided to deal with things in other ways.

This is where Padre Pio came right into the picture. It was around the time when his exhumation was taking place. I had heard of him, but I wasn't knowledgeable about him at that stage. I might have known about St. Bernadette, St. Francis or St. Martin because I knew of his magazine, but that was about it. Although I had heard the name Padre Pio, I wouldn't have known anything of any substance about him.

I also wasn't religious and I knew very little about the Catholic Church. I used to go to Mass, but I would make excuses whenever I could. I might say, 'I have to wash my hair' or whatever. If I didn't get to Mass, it didn't bother me. I didn't think that going to confession was necessary. I also didn't believe in miracles or magic cures.

Around that time, however, every newspaper I opened was featuring articles about Padre Pio because of the exhumation. People were talking about him with Joe Duffy on *Liveline* and with Gerry Ryan. The book *Padre Pio: The Irish Connection* had come out. I was in a bookshop and I felt compelled to pick it up. I thought, 'Who is this person? What's going on?' He was in my face, no matter where I turned. I read the book and thought, 'My God! He has done this for one person and that for another; I wonder would he be able to help me?'

One day, I was standing at home in my kitchen and I just started to cry. I was on my own. My wonderful husband was out at work and my kids were at school. I had never cried anything like it before. It was the most heart-wrenching, gut-wrenching sobbing you ever heard. I just couldn't stop and I didn't know what was happening. I had to lock the front and back doors in case anyone came in and heard me or saw me.

Suddenly, a voice came right into my head telling me to kill myself. I was going to commit suicide. That's basically what I was being told. I was answering back and saying, 'No, that's not like me. I'm not doing that.' The next thing I heard was, 'Only St. Pio can save you now!' It was said in a very different voice. I can't explain the voice: it was calm, although I can't say it was male or female. It's what saved me.

I remembered in the book it had mentioned the Irish Office for St. Pio. I rang directory enquiries and I got their number and telephoned them. I knew I had to get a relic of his because that's what I had read about in the book. I spoke, through my sobs, to a lady and I asked her where I could get a relic in the Midlands. She gave me a number of a man and he, in turn, gave me the number of a woman who had a mitten not far from where I lived.

I rang the woman and she asked me when I would be over. I said, 'Right away!' I drove, in floods of tears, and I cried the whole way over. I landed on her doorstep and she was a lovely woman. She brought me into her sitting-room and went out to get the relic, which was in a little case with a plastic cover over it. She then left me with it. Being as unreligious as I was at the time, I didn't know what to do with it. I was putting it on my head and placing it all over myself. I was blessing bits of me that were never blessed before.

Eventually, the lady came back in and we chatted about Padre Pio. She told me the story of how she came by the mitten. I then got up to leave. As I did so, I got a scent of roses at the door. It was like the smell that you would get from the freshest bunch of roses. It was the most wonderful smell you could ever imagine. It only hit me for a couple of seconds, but I knew what it was having read about it in the book.

I knew then that Padre Pio was looking after me and that everything was going to be OK. I drove straight to the nearby church. It was the first time in my life that I had genuinely gone into a church to pray. I knew I had to say thanks to Padre Pio. I went in and I prayed and I prayed and I prayed. Afterwards, I came back into my car and was on a high all the way home.

I don't have depression anymore and I have never looked back since. There wasn't an instant cure. Initially, I'd get up in the morning and say the Padre Pio prayer and that would get me through for some time. If I then felt a wave of depression coming on, I'd go down to my room and say the prayer again. Every time that I would say it, it reinforced my belief that all would be well. It gave me peace and helped me so much.

The depression is now gone completely. It disappeared quickly and, hand on heart, it doesn't affect me now. I must confess that, for some time, I took a natural remedy, although I never took prescription drugs. I only took the natural remedy for a few months, but I eventually threw it away. I think I was only using it as a crutch because I was afraid the depression would come back, but it hasn't.

Given what happened, I said to Padre Pio that I would go to San Giovanni to give thanks. I got the scent of roses while I was on that tour. It was a really powerful smell. I remember saying to my husband, 'Can you get the lovely smell of roses?' A girl in front of me heard me and said, 'That's another man's Rosary beads; they are scented.' Later, I said to the man, who was likewise on the tour, 'The smell of roses off your beads is extraordinary.' He just looked at me and said, 'Those beads aren't scented!'

I got the scent of roses at other times, too. The following year, I went to San Giovanni and the scent was hitting me in waves. Two of us got it, although another person didn't get it at all. It lasted the full length of the street. Sometimes, it would be faint; other times, it would be stronger. It was so powerful and lovely. I don't think it marks me out as being special, but I am sure it is Padre Pio. I think it is him letting me know that he is with me and looking after me.

My whole outlook on a lot of things in life has changed since what happened. I now go to Mass every day, if I can. If I don't go, I feel part of my day is missing. I feel blessed that we have the sacrament of confession; it's very important to me, maybe because of the importance Padre Pio attributed to it. I say my Rosary every day and I ask Padre Pio to pray for me. I probably don't pray to him as much as I should, but I try my best.

As a result, I don't fear anything anymore, especially death. I'm not scared about what comes after this life. It's not that I want to die now, but I know that this life is definitely not the end. I know, after we die, we will meet our Heavenly Father and all the saints, including Padre Pio. And I know it will be a better life after this one. I have no worries about that.

SARAH, FROM COUNTY DONEGAL, almost lost her baby son following his premature birth. It happened in 2008.

My son Harry was born 13 weeks early through an emergency Caesarean section. He weighed only one pound eight ounces. He was so small and fragile and his skin was transparent. He had light hair all over his little body because he wasn't fully developed. He was completely bruised and didn't look like a baby at all. To me, however, he was perfect.

He was born at 5.25 in the morning and he was taken to Dublin at 1 o'clock that afternoon. I only got to meet him for ten or 15 minutes. He had to go to Dublin to get the care he needed. I was very worried and emotional. I didn't know if I was coming or going. I wasn't able to travel in the ambulance with him because I was too weak. I felt horrible.

They were very concerned and said that he mightn't survive. They informed me, 'His lungs are extremely underdeveloped. It is touch and go. Take every minute as it comes.' Two days later, I got a call saying he wasn't going to make it and I needed to go up to him and be with him. They told me he had taken a brain haemorrhage. Although I was weak, I got a surge of energy and immediately got ready to go.

I travelled by ambulance to Dublin, along with my mum and my auntie. When I got there, my son recognised my voice and he moved. The doctors all remarked on it. But he was still in a bad way. I was told he had bled on both the left and right sides of the brain. The consultant spoke to us and said, 'He's had a major trauma and we can expect some side-effects.'

At the time, he was kept in an incubator in Intensive Care. There were tubes everywhere and he had to get seven blood transfusions because his blood count was extremely low. I was just numbed by what was happening and I felt I was in a bubble. I think I was suffering from shock and was crying a lot. I was angry and really couldn't understand why this was happening to me.

I was admitted to the hospital primarily because I was still in recovery. I had to have bed rest. Other than that, I was just up and down to my son. All that time, the doctors were still gloomy and told me, 'Stay strong, be there for Harry, talk to him and pray.' They got me prepared for the worst.

Back home, up in Donegal, word got out about my Harry. Everybody was talking about him and he was being prayed for at Mass. I don't know how he heard about him, but Bill Mc Laughlin, who possesses a relic of Padre Pio and who once miraculously survived a car crash thanks to his intercession, decided to come to visit Harry. He was only a few days in Dublin at that stage. We were all for it.

When Bill arrived at the hospital, he came up to my room. He introduced himself and shook our hands. He told us the story about his accident. He also told us about the mitt. He then asked us if he could go up to ICU. However, that was a big problem because parents and grandparents were only ever admitted to ICU two at a time. However, when they heard the Padre Pio mitt was arriving, they let the whole lot of us in.

In ICU, we prayed to Padre Pio along with Bill. We said a decade of the Rosary. Bill also produced the mitt. It was amazing because Harry moved the whole time all this was taking place. He had been barely moving before that; he had been mostly lifeless. Now, however, he was moving his tiny little arms and legs. It must have taken a lot for him to move at all; he was so small and weak. It was surreal.

We were in shock afterwards. I couldn't believe that Harry had moved so much. It was a big thing for us and we were so happy. Harry's granny, on his dad's side, was a very holy woman and she was saying, 'That's Padre Pio! That's him coming through!' She fully believed it was happening because of him. The rest of us did, too.

Immediately afterwards, Harry started getting much stronger and stronger. He still had his good days and bad days. He also had swelling of the brain; the fluid wasn't draining by itself and it had to be drained away. But he improved all the time, gaining weight and becoming more alert. His colour improved and he became more like a baby. Every time I went in, he would recognise my voice. I might speak first to the nurse and he would recognise me and move straight away and start looking.

Eventually, I came home to Donegal while Harry stayed in hospital up in Dublin. Overall, he stayed there for 11 weeks. I would go up and down by the bus. It was tough going. But he was getting better and better all the time. Some days I went up, I noticed that tubes had been removed. Things steadily improved.

Initially, he was in what's called ICU 1. Your aim was to get him into ICU 2, then into Special Care and the next move was home. One day, I went up to Dublin and walked into ICU 1, where his incubator should have been, but it wasn't there. I panicked and called a nurse. She said, 'Don't worry, he's in ICU 2.' I was thrilled and relieved. I was crying with happiness.

When Harry eventually came home, he weighed just over five pounds. It was the best day ever. I remember we brought him home in the car and I couldn't keep my eyes off him for the whole journey back to the house. I was nervous because he wouldn't have nurses and doctors around and I had no one to turn to if I wanted to ask a question. But, firstly, we got him used to his surroundings. Then, loads of people started to come to visit.

After he came home, he got stronger and bigger and better. Eventually, he became just like everybody else. We thought he'd be three months behind with everything, but he wasn't. He hit all his milestones. He was sitting up and crawling at the right time. He took his first steps and walked at the right time, too.

Since then, Harry has got bigger and stronger every day. He is now taller than average. He is just perfect. He is football-mad. He is an Arsenal fan and he loves Gaelic football as well. You never know, one day he might play for Donegal! He tells me he is going to be a fireman as well.

I believe that the arrival of the Padre Pio mitt changed everything for Harry. Beforehand, he was lifeless and we were getting prepared for the worst. He wasn't moving very much because of the brain haemorrhage. It was only when Bill arrived and we started praying that he really started moving. So I am 100 per cent sure there's a connection.

My belief about Padre Pio has changed totally because I have seen for myself what he can do. I know lots of people helped, including Harry's grandparents and his father, and there was help from me, too. But I think Padre Pio was the main helper, the miracle man. Even the paediatrician, every time he'd see Harry, would say, 'He is a miracle. I can't believe it.' I put it all down to Padre Pio.

EDEL, WHO IS BASED IN COUNTY KILDARE but who comes originally from County Donegal, experienced a dramatic recovery from a head injury after being blessed with Padre Pio relics. She was aged 27 at the time.

I had a bad fall in October 2008. It happened on a Saturday when I was visiting a cousin of mine in her house. I was going upstairs to the toilet and I suddenly fell backwards, down the stairs, onto a tiled floor at the bottom. I don't remember how it happened. I could have tripped, but they think I had a blackout. I have no recollection whatsoever.

From the damage that was done, it would seem that I had been quite near the top of the stairs when I fell and it was a long way down. I injured myself badly. I fractured my skull and my brain started swelling. It was probably a good thing that my skull was fractured; had it not been, there would have been no room for the brain to swell up and they would have had to operate to release the pressure. I was also unconscious.

My cousin came out and saw me crumbled at the bottom of the stairs. The ambulance was called and I vaguely remember the ambulance people attending to me. I also have some vague memories of being in the ambulance itself. I was quite scared and agitated and I was saying, 'I want to get up. Leave me alone.'

Eventually, we arrived at the hospital. My family was contacted and they were told it was very serious and to come to the hospital immediately. The staff clearly feared the worst. My family had to come from all over the place. A brother of mine was on top of a mountain in Spain. The moment he came down, he saw that he had a load of missed calls and the only person who hadn't called him was me, so he knew something was wrong with me.

By the following day, things weren't improving at all and I wasn't stabilising, so they decided to put me into an induced coma. From then on, it was basically a waiting game. My family had lots of meetings with the doctors and consultants, to keep on top of things, but the news still wasn't good. From what I heard later, I wasn't improving and everyone was at their wit's end.

A few days later, at 11 o'clock on the Wednesday morning, a relic of Padre Pio was brought in to me and some prayers were said. I don't remember anything about it. That evening, another relic was brought in. When he came out from being with me, the man with that relic, Bill Mc Laughlin, told my mother that I had lifted it and blessed myself with it. She said, 'That couldn't have happened. She's in a coma and she can't move.' However, he was definite that it did happen.

Everything started to improve after that. The response was instantaneous, from what I hear. I made a dramatic recovery. The following morning, they were saying, 'She's much better. We're going to take her out of the coma.' I came out of the coma, although I don't remember much about it. The first thing I remember was the Friday morning and all I wanted to do was go home.

I still had a lot of bruising on my neck and my head was sore, but I was able to walk and take a shower. Although I had fractured my skull and had been in a coma, the hospital staff said, 'It looks like you are OK now.' They felt that the best thing for me was to go home and rest and they said, 'We'll see how you do over the coming months.' So off I went home on the Sunday.

I think I was very lucky. Many people are kept in comas for weeks. I had only been in a coma from the Sunday to the Wednesday, which wasn't that long. I was also home in a week. The only thing that worried me was that I had put the family through such distress. It wasn't my fault, but I didn't want to see them being so upset. However, I was very grateful that everything had worked out and that I was OK.

Mum told me what had happened regarding Padre Pio and that I had blessed myself with the relic. She also told me how everyone was so shocked by how well I was and how there was so little damage. She said, 'Padre Pio saved your life.' Looking back, although I have suffered from tiredness and headaches and vertigo and things like that, I think she was right and I feel grateful that I was saved and given such mercy.

Later Years

I definitely believe there was some intercession on my behalf. I've always had a very strong faith and gone to Mass. Regarding Padre Pio, however, I couldn't say I had any connection with him; nor did my family. However, we were all religious and we asked for God's help. And there's no doubt the improvement took place after Padre Pio's relics were brought in.

Later, I went to San Giovanni to visit Padre Pio's tomb and to say thanks. It was something I felt I should do. I felt I owed him my life and I was very grateful for what had happened. I'm still thankful to him and I think he's amazing. He battled so many demons and had a hard life. But he was so humble, had a big heart and he was such a giving person. He certainly gave life back to me.

Mary, from County Meath, had a near-death experience in 2009, with Padre Pio appearing in the light at the end of the tunnel.

I developed a hernia in 2009. It perforated one Sunday night. I was in terrible pain down at the bottom of my stomach and I knew that I was in big trouble. I was roaring with the pain all night and I couldn't sleep. I stuck it out until the morning and I then went to the doctor.

I was sent by the doctor off to the hospital, where I stayed overnight, and I was then moved on to another hospital. They operated on me straight away. They found out that part of my bowel was gangrenous. I must have been very bad during the operation because they sent for my family.

Apparently, I stopped breathing and I was in a very serious way. They felt I was not going to make it and they wondered if they should turn off my machine. They didn't, however. It seems that a nurse had said, 'Don't turn it off. Why not give it another try?' And that's what they did.

At that stage, I travelled through a tunnel, a bit like the tube you go into when you get an MRI scan in hospital. It was a big silver tunnel and I went floating through it. When I came to the end of it, there was this huge light on each side. The light was very bright, like nothing I had ever seen before in my life. It was all around me and I was happy and at peace.

Padre Pio was at the end of the tunnel, sitting in the light. He was wearing white vestments with a pink colour around the sleeves. He had my little ten-month-old grandson folded in his arms. I had been minding him as his mother had gone back to work. Padre Pio said, 'You have to go back and rear your grandson.' With that, I started coming back.

I eventually came out of it, although I was in a coma and on a respirator for a full three months afterwards. In addition, I was unable to walk and I still can't do so to this day. They tried all sorts of exercises, but they didn't work. They also told me they had lost me during the operation and I was gone, so I am lucky to be alive and that's thanks to Padre Pio.

I wasn't surprised that Padre Pio had come to help me. I had been a big devotee of his for many years, probably from the ages of 18 or 19, which is over 50 years ago. I always felt he was an honest man and very holy. My mother and sisters always had great devotion to him, too. My sisters would have Masses in their houses in his honour. He was important to me and he still is.

I know he came to me that day of my operation, although, at one stage, when a priest was told that I had seen him in white vestments, he said, 'Padre Pio never dressed like that; he was always dressed in brown.' Later, however, I was given a picture of Padre Pio and he was wearing those exact same vestments. They were white with pink cuffs on the sleeves.

As a result of what happened, I can still look after my young grandson, who is now at school. I take him on Friday nights and on Saturday. I care for him, as Padre Pio told me to do. I also believe that Padre Pio is going to get me up and walking again, so I will never, ever give up.

I now have great devotion to Padre Pio and I have a medal of him around my neck. I wouldn't take it off my neck for all the tea in China. I know he looks after me. I always feel that my husband, who is dead, is on my left side and Padre Pio is on my right side, protecting me. He is always there by my side all the time. I am sure of that.

ADAM, FROM CORK CITY, recollects how he turned to Padre Pio after developing problems with his feet.

In 2009, when I was 21 years of age, I was experiencing all sorts of difficulties with my feet. I had swelling of the toes and sore heels and ankles. I was in a lot of pain and was walking with a hobble. Before that, I had gone over on my ankle and I thought it might have caused it. That had turned out to be a small hairline fracture in my left ankle, but it couldn't really explain my right foot, which was bad as well.

It progressed from there. I developed terrible troubles with my feet. I work in sales and the first thing I found myself explaining to people was why I was limping towards them, which is a very bad introduction. It was affecting me in lots of other ways, too, as I play a lot of football and squash. I wasn't able to play football for close to two years. It was like I was walking around with two cinder blocks attached to my feet.

I went to various hospitals and lots of different doctors. I was tested extensively and they were giving me injections with a two-inch or a three-inch needle into the heel. I was told it was potentially rheumatoid arthritis and that I was looking at a five-year pill programme. It was a lot to take in at the time, especially being so young. I do a lot of travelling, so that was bad news.

I tried lots of things, like alternative therapies, but was having no luck. I might have no pain for a week or two, but all of a sudden it would come back again. Just when I thought I was getting over it, it would be there once more. Things weren't great at all. It became very hard to put any weight on my feet and, in the morning, I'd have to pull myself down the banisters.

We are quite a religious family and my godfather is a believer in Padre Pio. He is very big into him. He's had his glove and stuff like that. He was asking me about what was wrong. I'm quite a spiritual person and believe in a higher being, although I wouldn't be one to go to Mass every week. However, I did have a mural of Padre Pio in my room, which I probably got from my godfather when I was young.

In times of hardship, you look for solace anywhere you can find it. I asked myself, 'What else, apart from all I'm trying, can help me?' I didn't want to take what the doctors said as being the be-all and end-all of it. I thought, 'I'm going down all these different paths trying to solve my problem, so why not try Padre Pio.' I turned to him to help me along.

I went to visit a man in Cork who is big into Padre Pio. He has relics and a statue. He has a lovely garden and my mother and I walked around it. He has a little prayer area, too, so we sat there praying for 15 or 20 minutes. He talked about the life of Padre Pio and mentioned his other devotees. It was a lovely time of the year when we went to him, so it was very memorable.

I wondered would any changes take place, not just straight away, but in the longer run. At that stage, it was about seven months after the whole thing had started. I was in bad shape at the time. Within the next two or three months, I could see some improvements in my feet. My feet started to slowly loosen out. I improved gradually. What was happening seemed like a blessing in disguise.

The improvements, although slow and gradual, were very noticeable. It felt like my feet broke free of a lot of shackles. It became easier to walk and I wasn't getting pains after doing it. There was less swelling and it was easier to get up in the morning. After about a month of walking, I was able to go to a gymnasium.

Believe it or not, the first night that I went back to the gym I was in a motorbike accident. I broke both my arms. That put me right back into the hospital scene for quite a while. It was straightforward broken bones and it was a case of letting them heal. Luckily, I was able to walk, although I couldn't use my arms for about six or seven months.

It took me roughly 15 months, overall, to get back to full mobility. I can now play squash and go kayaking and play football. The only thing I get now is the normal swelling in my feet following training. I realise now you take your feet and your hands for granted, but they are necessities. To have gone without them for such a long period of time, but now to be able to use them, is unbelievable.

I can't honestly say my recovery was linked to Padre Pio. All I can say is that during the times when I was looking for somebody to turn to and pray to, he was there and he was the person I eventually went to. It was a comfort for me to be able to pray and to turn to somebody and to ask for help to take away my pain. I didn't think anybody could do it, but it happened.

Although I can't directly say how the recovery occurred, I feel that somebody was looking over me and I was guided by somebody. I still have Padre Pio's picture up in the house. I don't really have anything else, although I do say the odd prayer. I'm not great at praying, but if I say one it's to him. He's always been part of my life and he's the man who took my pain.

JOAN, FROM COUNTY KERRY, outlines how Padre Pio was with her through her struggle with cancer.

Back in September 2009, I was diagnosed as having stage 4 ovarian cancer. About a year or two before that, I was caring for my mother-in-law, who has passed away since then. One morning, her home help came in and we were talking. I happened to mention that a priest was coming to town and was saying Mass and giving a talk about Padre Pio. It was Fr. Ermelindo, a Capuchin from San Giovanni who had looked after Padre Pio when he was alive. I said, 'I think I'll go.'

The home help, at that point, remarked, 'I'm looking after a woman who has a statue of Padre Pio and would love to get it blessed. Will you take it with you?' I said, 'Yeah, I'll take it, no problem.' So off I went to the Mass, carrying the statue with me. I went up to Fr. Ermelindo and he blessed it.

Afterwards, I remember saying, 'I'll get a statue of Padre

Later Years

Pio for myself.' The following Friday, I went off into town and found one in a shop. I brought it home and said, 'The priest will surely be around again next year and I'll get it blessed.'

Fr. Ermelindo came again the following year. I took the statue along to the church. A friend of mine was with me and she said, 'I had to laugh at you waltzing into the church with the statue under your arm.' I went to the local priest and asked him, 'Do you think Fr. Ermelindo will bless my statue?' He said, 'Of course he will.'

I went to Fr. Ermelindo and he did the blessing. There was a bigger Padre Pio statue on the altar at the time. I remember he said, 'It's not as big as the one on the altar, but it will do the very same thing,' and he put his hand on my forehead. I walked out, as happy as could be. Little did I know how much I would need Padre Pio when I was walking out with the statue that day!

In September 2009, I was admitted to the local hospital for an ultrasound. I was bloated and was gasping for breath. I had been bleeding earlier on in the year. I felt I wasn't well. The doctor said, 'You are full up with fluid. I'm not letting you go home; you wouldn't make it. You would actually die with a massive heart attack.' I was admitted straight away and they immediately took two litres of fluid from my lung cavity. They also put me on oxygen.

That was on a Tuesday. On Thursday morning, which was my birthday, the gynaecologist came in and said, 'The news is not good.' She said, 'You have stage 4 ovarian cancer.' You will need an operation, but it won't be done here; it will be done in Cork.' I said to her, 'How long have I got?' She said, 'You have six to eight weeks if you don't have an operation.'

It was an awful shock to be told you had cancer, especially

cancer of the highest stage. I went down under the clothes and started crying. Another lady, across from me, came over and she sat on the bed and said, 'I have this thing, too,' and she consoled me. My family came in and they also consoled me. I pulled myself together and off I went to Cork.

I travelled to Cork on the Friday and was admitted straight away. The oncologist said, 'All of the fluid will have to be drained off first and we will wait until the surgery is over and I will talk to you then.' He then said, 'You have a long road ahead of you, but with God's help we will get there.' They had to put in a drain through my back to bring out all the fluid. They couldn't give me an anaesthetic because the lung would deflate and, by God, did I feel it!

The water flew out, like they had just turned on a tap. The doctor drew out two basins of it. I was taken back to the ward, feeling very sore and very sorry for myself. I was there for a further week and they planned to take me off for surgery on the next Monday morning. Unfortunately, on the Monday, they came in and said, 'We can't take you for surgery because the fluid is building up again. It would be too dangerous.'

All of that time, I had my statue of St. Pio beside me. My husband had brought it up from Kerry. I had said to him, 'Wrap it in a towel for fear you might break it.' It stayed on my bedside locker the whole time. I was always looking at him and he was looking at me. I didn't pray to him because I couldn't pray; I had so much going on in my head. But I did say to him, 'I know you will help me.' At night, I would say to him, 'Please get me through another night.' I really felt he would and he always did.

Another woman from Kerry, who has passed away since, would come and take my statue to anyone that came in and say, 'That statue was blessed by the man who helped Padre Pio.' She would give everyone a big description. I said to her, 'You know, when I go off for my operation, you will have to babysit the statue.' I said, 'You will have to mind it to make sure it's OK!' And she did.

After two cancellations, and after being prepped twice, they eventually took me down for my surgery. It took place on 23 September, which was Padre Pio's anniversary. At 8.30 in the morning, I was brought down to theatre. I remember somebody asking me, 'Are you nervous?' I said, 'No, I'm not. I'm leaving it all in the hands of God and Padre Pio.'

I was operated on and then came back to Intensive Care at about five o'clock that evening. It was a big operation, which went on for four or five hours. After it, I had a lot of tubes left in and was given a morphine pump. The surgeon came in the next morning and he said, 'We're quite pleased with how it went.'

He asked me, 'How are you feeling?' I said, 'I'm doing alright, thanks be to God and his Blessed Mother and St. Pio.' He looked at me and said, 'Had I anything to do with it?' I replied, 'They guided your hands.' 'Oh, I give up!' he said. I really believe Padre Pio was with me, and the others as well.

I had my chemotherapy after that. It started on 28 October, which was my mother's birthday. I had it every three weeks up to 11 March. It was tough going. I was feeling very miserable and was very sick. I lost my hair and lost weight. I lost about three stone and couldn't eat. I fainted and passed out on the floor a few times.

There was one stage when I thought that I'd give up. My platelets had gone down and I was getting nosebleeds. I asked Padre Pio, 'Just give me the strength to keep going,' and he did. He was with me through that, too. His relic was always in my pocket. I'd take it out and look at it and rub it and ask him, 'Please get me through this.' I got there in the end.

I still go up to Cork every six months for a check-up. The last time I was there, they told me, 'We can't believe that you are still alive.' I asked, 'Why?' They said, 'The chances were only one in ten of ever meeting you again. People with stage 1 and stage 2 cancer are gone. You had stage 4 and it's a miracle you are here.' I replied, 'Thanks to Padre Pio and prayer.' I think they thought I was a right 'Holy Joe'!

They told me, 'We can never say you are 100 per cent cured. You could be in remission for years and it could come back, but we will see you every six months and we will keep checking you and see how it goes.' However, I am in remission now and I am feeling good and I rely on Padre Pio to make sure I never see the cancer again.

I think Padre Pio is wonderful and a saint of our time. I still pray to him. I say the Rosary, which was one of his favourites. I carry his relic in my pocket every day. I even have a relic of him in my pocket at the moment and there's one in my bag. I have a candle on the table, with a little stand, and his picture is on it. I go to the Padre Pio prayer meetings.

Of course, his statue is still beside my bed. I think that I was meant to get it blessed. It was almost like fate. The statue I bought was even the only one left in the shop when I went in. I think it was meant to be. As a result, when the cancer came, I always knew I had St. Pio beside me, helping me along the way.

Later Years

Noel, from County Clare, reflects on how a potentially disastrous Padre Pio event he was attempting to organise was saved.

I developed an interest in Padre Pio when I was in my early 20s. There was something about him. He had a great love of Irish people because Ireland was the first country outside of Italy to recognise his gifts. From the 1950s onwards, people went over to see him and he knew they were genuine. They brought thousands of requests. They were poor and had a love of Our Lady, and he liked that.

The love of Padre Pio was in my family. My father was a devotee of his. He had Parkinson's and suffered badly. I used to see him down on his bony legs, praying away to Padre Pio. Because of his illness, he would half-forget the prayers. It was sad, but uplifting, to watch.

I used to take my father for coffee every morning, until he became much too unwell to go. One morning, after he stopped, a lady came over to me and said, 'I notice your father doesn't join you for coffee anymore. I reckon he must be ill.' I said, 'That's right.' 'Look,' she said, 'I'm Church of Ireland and I have this little present for your father.' She handed me a Padre Pio relic. He was absolutely thrilled, especially considering that a Church of Ireland person had given it to him.

My brother also had great devotion to Padre Pio and brought a man who had one of his relics around to sick people. I became intrigued by what he was doing. He was only in his late 20s and I was even younger, in my earlier 20s. At the time, I was working in a job that required me to go around and visit houses. I noticed that so many people had Padre Pio's picture up on their walls, alongside John F. Kennedy and the Pope. Everybody loved him.

I eventually opened up my house in County Clare in the

name of Padre Pio and ran healing and conversion courses. On one occasion, in 2010, I decided to bring a relic there. No one could help me at the time. Eventually, one person said, 'I have a first-class relic, no problem. Pick it up on Friday.' As a result, I went about organising things. Word spread everywhere that the event was being held on the Saturday.

I must have got 200 or 300 calls from people. They were planning to come from as far away as Dundalk and from Drogheda. On the Wednesday, I was in Tralee and a lady said to me, 'I'm getting ready to travel to a Padre Pio event on Saturday.' She didn't know it was I was the person who was organising it. People seemed to be coming from far and wide.

When I called for the relic on the Friday, all the person had was a tiny, microscopic dot of a relic on a card. I was in a state of turmoil and shock. It was 2.30 in the afternoon and I was panicking. I didn't know what to do. I drove around in my car and ended up in a car park on the Dublin road. I parked there, panic-stricken, and I had a chat with Padre Pio. I talked to him and asked him for help.

The next thing, the phone rang. It was a woman telling me, 'I just want to let you know that I can't make it tomorrow.' I said, 'Don't worry. Anyway, I don't know what I'm going to do because I have no relic.' She said, 'Oh, my goodness! You should go out and visit a man named Tom Cooney; he met Padre Pio in the 1960s.' I didn't know anything about him, but I decided to pay a visit and ask his advice and see what he might suggest.

I drove to his house and he answered the door. I asked him, 'Are you the man who met Padre Pio?' He said, 'I am.' I said, 'I'm in terrible trouble and I need help.' He brought me down into his kitchen and I then told him everything. Eventually, he asked me, 'Would you like to see a Padre Pio mitten?' He produced this brown leatherette bag and in it was a relic in a plastic cover. He also had a stigmata bandage.

I knew I couldn't ask the man for a loan of them. I also knew he was an old man and would find it hard to travel. But I asked him if he would come. He said, 'No, no, no, I can't.' However, there was a picture of Padre Pio on the wall and I was looking at it and I knew he wouldn't let me down. Tom eventually said, 'Give me a call tomorrow, at 10.30, and I'll see.' I immediately changed from a state of turmoil to a state of hope.

I called to Tom's house at 10.30 the next morning and he was ready to travel. On the journey, he told me about all the people – including priests and bishops – that he had turned down. He named them all. He said, 'Despite that, I just could not say no to you. I wanted to, but I couldn't.'

When we arrived in Kilkee, the whole place was packed. I don't think there's ever been a traffic jam in the town, but there was on that day. There were Guards out in their fluorescent jackets. I thought it was either because of a funeral or because they were checking for tax and insurance. I said to one Guard, 'What's going on?' He turned to me and said, 'It's your fault. They are all going to your place.'

About 700 or 800 people were there. They were packed for about 200 or 300 yards up the street. We started at about two o'clock. Tom Cooney took out his relics and he gave a testimony. People were blessed with the relics and we said prayers. We had a priest there hearing confessions. The priest told me afterwards, 'I think I heard more confessions than I did in an entire year in my parish. It was truly inspiring.' People stood up and told their stories. The whole thing went on until about 8.30 that evening. It was a really powerful event.

I really believe Padre Pio directed things that day. I think he saw what had happened and he blessed the event. I think he saw the turmoil I was in and he knew I was genuine. First of all, there was the woman who rang me. Then there was Tom Cooney, who I never heard of before. Tom also agreed to do it against the odds. I think Padre Pio stepped in and made it all happen.

I am a devotee of Padre Pio to this day. I talk to him all the time. I treat him and Jesus as best friends and I talk to them as friends. I ask his advice. Sometimes, I might get cross and say, 'You let me down badly there.' But I know he listens. He is like a father figure. He may not always give me what I want, just like a father may not give children sweets because they would destroy their dinner, but you have to trust him and believe he knows what is best for you.

To this day, I bring Padre Pio relics out to people who wouldn't go near priests or a church. No matter how tough they are, or how hostile they are, I always find that they ask me to come in whenever I say, 'I have a Padre Pio relic here. Would you like to be blessed with it?' Travellers love him as well; their faith in him is genuine and real. Everyone adores him, rich and poor. They know he loves them and is sincere. No one shuts the door on you when you mention Padre Pio.

KATHLEEN, FROM COUNTY KERRY, recalls how Padre Pio helped her nephew overcome a brain tumour.

My nephew Dylan, who is also my husband's godchild, got sick in 2011. He was seven years old at that stage. He came home from school one day after Christmas and he felt ill. He was vomiting and had a pain in his head. There were other children getting sick and we thought it might have been a bug. However, about a week later, he felt bad again.

Dylan was, and is, a lovely boy, mad for football and great fun. He loves the Kerry football team and Manchester United. We don't have any children of our own, but he would visit us from when he was very small. We live very near him. He was always mad to come over to us. We loved having him because he was a breath of fresh air.

His sickness started to worry us, however, after it went on for two or three weeks. It was suggested that maybe he was being bullied at school. His mother went over to the teacher. She said, 'No way.' He was popular with the other kids. He was doing well and was very quick to pick things up. He was performing well at his tests. He had also never created any fuss about going to school. The teacher said she would keep her eye on things.

One Friday evening, at about five minutes to three, he was about to come home from school and he got sick again. The teacher rang his mum. He was taken to the doctor, who said, 'It's more than a bug. We'll have to investigate.' He was sent to the local hospital and they did tests including an MRI scan. He was in wonderful form in the hospital, where he stayed overnight, and was delighted with his visitors. It was all a bit of a novelty. Unfortunately, the result was bad and he had a tumour in the brain. The tumour was the size of a mandarin orange.

The following morning, they sent him up to the Children's Hospital in Dublin. They did scans there as well. They then said, 'There's a long road of chemotherapy and radiotherapy ahead.' They told us he would need an operation, too. They also said,

'Some children make it and some children don't.' Everything was so uncertain. If they had said, 'After six months, or a year, or two years, he will be grand,' we would have felt fine. But the uncertainty was terrible.

He went off up to Dublin on a Thursday and he then had the operation on the Friday morning. We were absolutely devastated and in bits. We couldn't sleep a wink. He was the same as a child of our own and we were very worried. Someone suggested that we should contact the Irish Office for St. Pio and the lady very obligingly came in with Padre Pio's glove. She let us have it for half an hour while she waited in the lobby. We put it under his pillow and we prayed so hard to Padre Pio, looking for help.

The operation went very well. They told us that they had taken away 80 per cent of the tumour and they were hoping the chemotherapy and radiotherapy would get rid of the rest of it. He then came back home to Kerry and had to wait before the other treatments could start. It was a very tough time.

Prior to the chemotherapy, my brother got in contact with another man, from Cork, who came to us with the Padre Pio glove. He came to the house on several occasions. He would have Dylan touch the glove. He gave him pictures and spoke to him as well. We prayed to Padre Pio, asking for help. We prayed so hard, not only to him but to the Sacred Heart. I would also say to Our Lady, 'You were a mother, too, and I know you went through so much. Be with our little baby.'

My nephew eventually went back up to Dublin and he had radiotherapy for 30 days, over six weeks. He then had four rounds of chemotherapy. It was an extremely difficult time. The chemotherapy made him very sick. He lost weight. He had lovely blond hair and he lost it after a few rounds. It wasn't bad when the hair was gone, but it was awful when it was going. The first week, he was so, so tired that he couldn't lift a finger. He dealt with the rest of it very well. He was lively and in good form and he still had energy.

All that time, we relied on Padre Pio. When the treatment started to go well, we would say, 'Thanks be to God! Padre Pio and the Sacred Heart are looking after us. They are getting us through it.' We were marking off the days and calling on Padre Pio to stay by Dylan's side. He must have stayed with him because he got through things very well. I think Padre Pio and the Sacred Heart were with him all the way.

The treatment eventually came to an end. His first check-up was at the beginning of December. They were happy with him, although there was a lot of scarring after the operation. He was doing exactly as well as he should be doing. Every three months after that, he was back for another check-up and everything was fine.

He put weight back on again. His hair started growing. He became taller and his coordination improved, which was very important. Another boy who had something similar ended up having special needs, so Dylan was extremely lucky. He also returned to school and, only last Friday, he got ten out of ten in his Irish test. He's in great form, playing football and basketball and, of course, supporting Kerry!

I'm certain that Padre Pio played a major role in Dylan's recovery. I think he is very powerful and a great intercessor. I have read so many stories of people who have been cured by him and touched by him. He has cured people who have been very, very sick. I think he did the same for us. Every day Dylan walks in our door from school, or kicks the ball up and down the hall, or goes to get something to eat, I realise what Padre Pio has done. I thought I would never see those days again.

I now talk to Padre Pio every day, the same way that I'm talking to you. I have him in my prayer book, with his picture and a relic. I know he looked after us and I always ask him to take care of us. I pray to him every night that Dylan will do well at school and get through his lessons. I also pray that he will go on to have a good and healthy life and that we will never hear about the tumour again.

DAVE, FROM COUNTY CORK, describes Padre Pio's role in his son's recovery from a serious assault.

It all started on a Bank Holiday morning in 2011. I remember it was a dirty, wet day and I was at home. I rarely do the shopping, but my wife was going and I said to her, 'I'll go with you. I have nothing else to do.' All my normal hobbies and pastimes were out of the question because of the bad day. It was around 11 o'clock in the morning.

When I was in the supermarket, I got a phone call from my son's girlfriend, who said that he had been assaulted the night before and he had been admitted to hospital. A person had pulled a punch on him and struck him to the ground. His head hit the footpath and he was unconscious.

By the time we got over to the hospital, he hadn't regained consciousness. For us, it was horrific to see him because he wasn't responding. It was clear that he was in bad condition. They weren't worried about life or death, but they were very worried about the serious nature of the brain injury itself. Eventually, he had a scan and it showed up that things were bad. They didn't know if he would need surgery or what they would do.

They moved him to another hospital, where he could be seen by a neurosurgeon. They informed us there that they weren't going to operate. They said, 'The pressure in his brain is high, but we will give it time to resolve itself as opposed to doing anything to relieve it.' They took him to Intensive Care and put him in an induced coma. From then on, they monitored his brain pressure, which was fluctuating.

He remained in that induced coma for about a week. He had tubes coming out of him and machines all around. At one stage, they told us the level of pressure on his brain that they needed to stabilise him. It might have been a mistake telling us that because every time we went in to see him our hearts were in our mouths. We were checking to see if it was going too high and worried that he would need surgery.

Padre Pio came into the picture at that early stage. A good friend of my wife had said, 'Look, I know somebody who has a relic of Padre Pio. Would you like it to be brought to your son?' We are Catholics and go to Mass, although we are not especially religious or devout, but we said, 'We would love that.' In times of crisis, you cling on to anything you can get.

My wife and I knew of Padre Pio at the time. I had heard about him from my grandmother and mother as I grew up. He was very well-known in our family. I knew of the bleeding hands and knew quite a bit about him, although I wouldn't have read about him a lot. I would also have heard about the glove and his healing powers.

This man came in with the relic of Padre Pio. I remember my son was still in an induced coma, in Intensive Care, when he arrived. He prayed with my son and touched him with the glove. I can't say that something immediately took place, but I believe that what happened helped us a lot. The visit was important and significant for us and I believed something might come out of it.

A few days later, after about a week in hospital, they turned off the machines and took him out of the induced coma. He was allowed to breathe on his own. He started to move. It would start with a hand and then a leg. Initially, we felt that one side wasn't responding and that was worrying, but it resolved itself. Although he still couldn't talk or communicate, things started to look a bit better.

It took maybe eight days for him to open his eyes and he was then brought out into the ward. He was alert, at that stage, but he became quite aggressive and didn't know what he was doing. He constantly paced up and down the ward. He kept saying, 'Come on. I want to go home. I want to get out of here.' He still didn't know any of us and couldn't identify us. He didn't converse. He also didn't call any of us by name and that continued for the best part of another three weeks.

It took until the fourth week for my son to come around and he was eventually released from hospital. He can now walk and talk, no problem. He has gone back to work on a modified basis. However, he is still dealing with his injuries and everything that happened. He still has memory lapses and can mix up some words. But it takes the brain a long time to recover and whether he will ever fully get back to himself, I don't know.

Since it happened, we always pray to Padre Pio. We never had a photograph of him in our home, but we now have one up; it's there when you come down the stairs. I carry his relic in my wallet. We regularly go to Mass, and always did, and my son has started going back to Mass as well, which is nice.

I think that Padre Pio was an unusual character. Before my family got into trouble, I would have been sceptical about him and I still don't know how he does what he is supposed to do. But he was a person who meant something to me and a person I could pray to. It was important to have somebody like him there at the time.

I wouldn't say that what happened was a miracle, but I do believe that he helped us. I felt that at the time; that something was helping us. One way or the other, we are very grateful for where we are and so is my son. If you had said to me that day the man came in with the relic that we'd be where we are now, I would have bitten your hand off.

MARY, FROM COUNTY DUBLIN, talks about some immensely powerful Padre Pio mementoes which were given to her in recent years.

I was given photographs of Padre Pio which are very important to me. I got them in County Kerry. They are photographs taken in 1945, in San Giovanni Rotondo, by a man named Herbst. He was an officer in the U.S. Army, who was stationed in Italy during World War II and who eventually settled in County Kerry. He got an invitation to the monastery in San Giovanni during the closing days of the war. The invitation was to attend a Mass said by Padre Pio.

He attended the Mass and he took four photographs there, which are now very faded and very brown. I don't know what kind of camera he had, but they are very dark, old-fashioned pictures. Padre Pio is lifting the Blessed Sacrament and chalice in one of them. He is putting his head down in another. He is saying the last part of the Mass in a third. In the last one, he is raising his hand at the elevation of the sacred host.

He is not wearing any gloves and the stigmata in his open hands are very visible. You can see the holes in his hands, both back and front. His hands are pure raw. Mr. Herbst's wife,

Joan, brought the photos to a healing Mass I attended in Kerry. The moment I placed my hand on the photographs, heat emanated from them. When other people put their hands on the pictures, intense heat emanated, too. Mrs. Herbst gave the photographs to me and I am very honoured to have them.

I have the photos inside a frame, under a light. I take the frame out every day and I put my hand on the photos. Any time I do that, I feel the heat. I'm getting it now as I speak to you. It's burning the hand off me. Other people have felt the heat, too. I then pray to Padre Pio for lots of things, including other people. I pray to him three times a day and I think he cares for me.

Sometimes, I can smell Padre Pio's perfume from the photographs. It's a very strong, intense smell of roses. I don't use perfume, but I get the beautiful aroma of roses drifting by. It's like the wonderful smell you would get off those organic roses years ago in gardens. I don't get it often; mainly when I'm sitting down and crying and doing a lot of worrying.

I can be very angry, especially when things go badly wrong. I might ask God, 'Why me?' But I think we shouldn't ask God that. When that happens, I find Padre Pio says, 'Look, Mary, I'm looking after you,' and I get this great smell of perfume. I believe the smell goes into my soul and the worry disappears. I then get up and I forget that whatever was worrying me has ever happened.

I also have a first-class relic of Padre Pio, which is 75 years old. It's a piece of his clothing on a small picture. I got it through a woman whose aunt was a nun and who sent it to her from overseas. I brought it to prayer meetings, hoping to heal people. One very young girl, aged seven, who had been diagnosed with arthritis, was told by doctors that she would be on medication for the rest of her days. I prayed with her and she is fine to this day.

I believe Padre Pio is a great man and a great healer. He was very holy, a wonderful saint who bore the stigmata of Our Lord. He could do so many things: appear anywhere and look into your soul and see what you were thinking. He was a fantastic person, had a hard life, which I have had, too, and I think he helps me. Every time I'm in trouble or upset, I just pray to him. He will help you any time you do that.

I say the Rosary every morning and I pray to Our Lord, St. Anthony, St. Joseph, St. Martin and Our Lady, who won't refuse you anything and who will go to her son for you. But I also always pray to Padre Pio. He gives me great strength to endure things I have had to put up with. And I believe I have experienced the great healing and the great peace that he had in his own heart.

At the end of the day, we are not our own masters. We all depend on Jesus and Mary and we depend on the saints. We also depend on Padre Pio. I could never afford to go to San Giovanni, to where he lived and died, but I don't think you have to go. Instead, Padre Pio comes to me. I think he is here, around me. He is everywhere and whatever he decides for me, I will accept it.

ACKNOWLEDGEMENTS

This book was inspired by a visit some years ago to the Capuchin Day Centre for Homeless People, located in Bow Street, Dublin. There can be few charities with a more genuinely Christian ethos, providing food and day-care facilities to people who are vulnerable and in need.

That the centre has become so well-known reflects the grim times we live in; that it is run so impressively is due to the staff and especially its founder Brother Kevin Crowley. The proceeds from the sale of this book will hopefully help it to continue its wonderful work.

Many people have been pivotal in getting this project off the ground, most notably Jerry O'Sullivan from County Cork. Through his work on behalf of Padre Pio, he put me in contact with many of the people whose stories are in the book. I am extremely grateful for his support.

Others who made valuable contributions include Gemma Dillon, Bill Mc Laughlin, Brendan Byrne, Patricia Comiskey and Helen Keane, to whom I am indebted. I would also like to thank Vera, from County Down, who provided valuable insights to the saint's aroma of sanctity. Likewise, Fr. James Grace's assistance was much appreciated.

As always, Linda Monahan, from Typeform, did sterling work on the cover, while Pat Conneely put in long hours laying out the text. Two books proved to be most useful – *Wings on the Cross* by Fr. P. Hamilton Pollock and *South to*

Acknowledgements

Sicily by Seán O'Faoláin, both of which are long out of print. Seán O'Faoláin's visit to Padre Pio is also featured in the May 1953 edition of *The Irish Digest*.

In particular, my gratitude goes to Úna O'Hagan for nurturing this project from beginning to end. She put in many untold hours, reading the stories, vetting the text and devising the structure and shape of the book. Without her help, this venture would never have come to fruition.

Finally, I would like to thank the contributors for their wonderful stories. They were a pleasure to work with and their accounts were always sincere. They have done a great service in keeping alive interest in, and devotion to, Ireland's favourite saint, Padre Pio.

ALSO FROM CAPEL ISLAND PRESS

GOING HOME

IRISH STORIES FROM THE EDGE OF DEATH

Colm Keane

Going Home contains the most comprehensive insights ever provided by Irish people into what happens when we die.

Many of those interviewed have clinically died – some after heart attacks, others after long illnesses or accidents. They have returned to claim – 'There is life after death!'

Most have travelled through dark tunnels and entered intensely bright lights. Some have been greeted by dead relatives and met a superior being. All have floated outside their bodies and watched themselves down below.

Those left behind describe visions of relatives who passed away. The book also acquaints us with the latest scientific research.

Award-winning journalist Colm Keane has spoken to people from all corners of Ireland and recounts their stories.

Based on years of research, Going Home provides us with the most riveting insight we may ever get into where we go after death.

Reviews of *Going Home*

'Fascinating' *Irish Daily Mail*
'Intriguing' *Sunday World*
'A beautiful, satisfying, comforting book' *Radio Kerry*

ALSO FROM CAPEL ISLAND PRESS

THE DISTANT SHORE
MORE IRISH STORIES FROM THE EDGE OF DEATH

Colm Keane

The Distant Shore is packed with a wealth of new Irish stories about life after death.

Extraordinary accounts of what takes place when we die are featured throughout. Reunions with deceased relatives and friends, and encounters with a 'superior being', are included.

Visions of dead family members are described. The book also examines astonishing premonitions of future events.

This compilation was inspired by the huge response to Colm Keane's number one bestseller Going Home – a groundbreaking book that remained a top seller for six months.

Containing new material and insights, The Distant Shore is indispensable reading for those who want to know what happens when we pass away.

Reviews of *The Distant Shore*

'Amazing new stories' *Irish Independent*

'Terrific, wonderful read' *Cork 103 FM*

'A source of genuine comfort to anyone who has suffered a bereavement' *Western People*

ALSO FROM CAPEL ISLAND PRESS

FOREWARNED

EXTRAORDINARY IRISH STORIES OF PREMONITIONS AND DREAMS

Colm Keane

Did you ever have a feeling that something bad was going to happen? Perhaps you dreamt of a future event? Maybe you had a 'gut feeling' that an illness, death, car crash or some other incident was about to occur?

Most Irish people, at some time in their lives, have experienced a forewarning of the future. It may reveal itself as a sense of unease. Alternatively, it may be more intense and involve a terrifying foreboding. Perhaps it brings good news.

Forewarned is the first Irish study of this intriguing phenomenon. Crammed with fascinating stories, the book also presents the latest scientific evidence proving that the future is closer to our minds than we think.

Reviews of *Forewarned*

'Amazing stories' *Belfast Telegraph*

'Authenticity of experience is written all over these reports' *Irish Catholic*

'A fascinating read' *Soul & Spirit*

ALSO FROM CAPEL ISLAND PRESS

WE'LL MEET AGAIN

IRISH DEATHBED VISIONS
WHO YOU MEET WHEN YOU DIE

Colm Keane

We do not die alone. That's the remarkable conclusion of this extraordinary book examining deathbed visions.

Parents, children, brothers, sisters and close friends who have already died are among those who return to us as we pass away. Religious figures appear to others, while more see visions of beautiful landscapes.

Riveting case histories are featured, along with numerous stories from those left behind who describe after-death visitations and other strange occurrences. The latest scientific evidence is discussed.

We'll Meet Again, written by award-winning journalist Colm Keane, is one of the most challenging books ever compiled on this intriguing theme.

Reviews of *We'll Meet Again*
'A total page-turner' *Cork 103 FM*
'Packed with riveting case histories' *LMFM Radio*
'A fascinating book' *Limerick's Live 95FM*

Capel Island Press
36 Raheen Park, Bray, County Wicklow, Ireland
Email: capelislandpress@hotmail.com